Praise

'Deriving value from data is imperative to data professionals and organisations. Unfortunately, organisations may still struggle to find the value they should through their data investments. In their book, *Drive RAPPID Results From Data*, Zjaén and Karl provide a framework to empower organisations to gather data and find value. Don't just guess at the value you bring, implement a way to drive it. This book will help you find the insights you need to help your organisation find more value from its data.'
— **Jordan Morrow**, The Godfather of Data Literacy

'There are many books focused on the amazing potential of data and analytics. However, they often leave the reader excited but without a usable path on how to get there. Apart from being a fun and easy read, this book introduces an easy-to-follow framework to design a sustainable data and analytics roadmap to deliver continuous value. Going further, Karl and Zjaén provide practitioners with online collaborative tools and ability to share challenges and experience with a community of interest to progress faster. If you want to take data and analytics beyond the hype, this book will help you get there.'
— **Dr Alex Rummel** (PhD in AI), CEO, Slipstream Data

'This essential book guides leaders on becoming data-value-driven. During my research with 100+ Data, Analytics and AI Leaders in 2023 and 2024, I found their main challenges to be cultural, not technological. Business buy-in and adoption are crucial. Data, analytics and AI leaders are doing their best to speak the language of business. But business leaders must better understand how to generate value from data. Packed with practical advice, recipes, and frameworks, this book helps business, IT, and data, analytics and AI leaders converge at the intersection of data's economic value. I am excited to use and share it.'

— **Debbie Botha**, member of the D^3 Institute Industry Council at Harvard Business School, Managing Director of Dalebrook Media Middle East

'This book is interesting, enjoyable but most importantly useful. Lots of practical advice and frameworks to make it easy for you to follow. Read it once to get the overview then ingest the chapters that will help you most now!'

— **Caroline Carruthers**, author of *The Chief Data Officer's Playbook*, Chief Executive of Carruthers and Jackson

'By prioritising a value-driven approach over a purely data-centric one, this book skilfully translates complex technical concepts into relatable narratives, making the journey from data to business value accessible to a wide audience. Instead of overwhelming the reader with technical details, Zjaén and Karl combine conventional approaches with modern data-driven strategies using practical, ready-to-implement frameworks. I can see immediate applications for this valuable content in my data-related postgraduate courses, exploring advanced analytics and its business implications. This book is an essential guide for leaders, professionals, and educators looking to confidently navigate – and teach – the evolving landscape of data analytics.'

— **Prof. Hanlie Smuts**, Chair of School of Information Technology, University of Pretoria

'Any industry or company that wants to remain relevant and still be in business in the near future will need to get to grips with the world of data and everything it has to offer. To future-proof your business for this new world where data and AI will have a life-changing impact, I would highly recommend reading this book.'

— **Andrew Murgatroyd**, CEO, Aztomix (TopShopper), non-executive director of JSE-listed technology group

'In a rapidly evolving world, teeming with new information and growing consumer demands, the need for swift decision-making and value delivery is paramount. This book readily outlines the crucial

framework for advancing your organisation's data maturity and aligning your capabilities to support this growth. The authors' insights into data value leadership underscore its priority in today's business landscape.'
  — **Phenyo Molefe**, IT and Digital BSS/OSS Transformation, MTN

'This book is a must-read for any business leader looking to unlock the full potential of their data analytics journey. The book provides a comprehensive guide to navigating the complexities of data analytics, with practical frameworks and real-life examples that enable readers to confidently invest in high-value data analytics initiatives. The insights and guidance provided in this book are invaluable for any company looking to drive growth and gain a competitive edge through data analytics.'
  — **Dominic Albrecht**, Head of Analytics, Digital Planet

'I was hooked from page one! This book is packed with practical value, and its short, dense chapters make it a quick and impactful read. The authors' experience shines through as they anticipate and address readers' questions. I appreciated how the book speaks to different personas, from CDO to CEO to CFO, highlighting the shared importance of data. A truly pragmatic guide, I walked away with actionable ideas to test and implement. A must-read!'
  — **Emmanuel Kalunga**, Data Science – AI and Insight Lead, BCX

'This book is a standout guide that transforms the daunting task of leveraging data analytics into a clear and actionable journey. The authors' deep expertise is evident through the practical frameworks and methodologies they introduce. These tools are not only insightful but are also designed for immediate implementation, offering readers a structured path to data-driven success. What sets this book apart is its holistic approach. The emphasis on being value-driven rather than merely data-driven is a crucial perspective that ensures alignment with business goals and long-term success.'

— **Shradha Samantray**, Senior Director of Data and Analytics, Informa

'Your insights into bridging the gap between traditional methodologies and modern data-driven approaches were nothing short of transformative for me. You have not just simplified the overwhelming complexities of scaling AI and data automation; you have taken us back to the foundational principles that ensure sustainable success. In a time where technology evolves faster than we can sometimes comprehend, your ability to ground these advancements in clear, actionable frameworks is visionary.'

— **Veronica Brits**, Founder and CEO, FeedFlex Creatives

'The writing style is masterful, using relatable stories to set the tone for complex technical concepts. This approach makes the reading experience both enjoyable and accessible, allowing readers to easily connect the dots between the narrative and the technical content. This book is invaluable for all leaders – offering confidence to those delivering data analytics value, and empowering those who need to define and contract their data analytics requirements to drive business improvement.'

— **Khumbudzo Mashamba**, Manager: Data and BPM, Old Mutual South Africa

FOREWORD BY RANDALL ABRAHAMS

DRIVE

RAPPID

REULT

FROM DATA

A proven methodology for business leaders to confidently unlock data-led growth

ZJAÉN COETZEE &
KARL DINKELMANN CA(SA)

Re think

First published in Great Britain in 2025
by Rethink Press (www.rethinkpress.com)

DISCLAIMER

To our teams of data professionals

This book would not have been possible without your years of hard work and dedication to our collective cause.

To you, the business leader who will read this book

Keep taking brave steps towards becoming a data-confident leader, driving data analytics-led value for your company.

Contents

Foreword

Randall Abrahams, media personality, digital executive and innovation thought leader

I have a sense that everyone in search of an ounce of inspiration and in possession of a decent internet connection will eventually make use of AI, either via a simplified version through the Meta platform or by utilising one of the many copilots floating in the ether. The very term *AI* has become so absolute, all-encompassing, dominant and, at the same time, generic. On the one hand, AI is offered up as a liberator offering salvation, while just a fleeting glance in the opposite direction delivers what many view as a terminal blow. As we survey the illimitable data vista, we must appreciate that the old world of *big data* – an impact felt just over a decade ago – lies in stark contrast to the new world of AI. The latter sphere has experienced a groundswell among those for whom a deep understanding and appreciation of data sets is inconsequential and unnecessary. The outcome therefore matters.

Let us revert to inspiration for a moment. I sit in South Africa, on the eve of an important political election, wondering just what level of data analytics the various parties have employed, how deployment was managed and ultimately where the respective parties will find value (quite different from where they *believe* they will find value). Crucially, this is not a question of *if*.

Data is simply everywhere – like Taylor Swift on her way to reenergising a monoculture. It is data and not Dallas (1970s/80s CBS television soap opera staple) that has tongues wagging around the water cooler. The big questions are what we do with data and, in the final analysis, what data can do for and to us. (The solid question around Dallas at the time was 'Who shot JR?') Data becomes an integral part of conversations as deep and wide as Hollywood, Messi and Musk to the banking and investment systems that underpin Western capitalism. Big data has succumbed to the minutiae, integration and consolidation that is AI; AI is so much more than a watchword as it swiftly outstrips the usage rate for TikTok. If that does not turn your head about data, best return this book to the shelf.

Now for the challenge – or rather, the series of challenges – enveloping the world of data mapping, governance and administration.

What exactly is valuable data, and how can pinpointing value lead to value creation?

What is the journey from prized to profitable?

While the executives and teams who manage data inside companies understand and appreciate the considerable weight of their direct environment, are they equipped to navigate the trajectory to unlocking value? They run the very real risk of becoming gatekeepers, not being mindful of building relationships with those whose jobs revolve around driving revenues and shareholder value.

At what inflection point does a CEO take a definitive step towards making data value unlock part of the dividend strategy?

None of these questions bear easy answers, and managing a course towards every layer of a company making data a central part of its strategy is a lot harder than it sounds. Both vision and investment are mandatory just to begin with, and most things in life that have long-term positive outcomes also require ongoing engagement and staying the course. CEOs, CFOs, CDAOs do not remain at companies for a lifetime anymore. This is why ensuring that each layer of a company understands its own data orbit is so critical.

This book does not provide a rudimentary step-by-step guide like the self-help genre that all too often offers a magical path to self-realisation. I use the term *magical* here, because if you really believe in ten-step guides, any sleight-of-hand card trick will work. The world of data is far too labyrinthine and complex, and in the pages of this book we have yet another stratum: *data value unlock*. Every dataset is unique, and so too is every company structure and the individuals who fill those positions. This book offers an essential map towards simply getting a handle on things and moving briskly to making transformative decisions. Again, I am doing the best job I can of underselling what lies within the following chapters. Dimensions for consideration are both plentiful and diverse. This is a book to be read, digested and reread. Your task is achieved only once its pages are illuminated with Post-its and with notes in pencil. Then the real work begins.

Introduction

We start with a story that puts the complexities of driving data analytics-led value into perspective.

When Karl was 18, he went on holiday with friends to a wildlife reserve. One afternoon, following some poolside antics, he dived in, not realising that the pool was only waist-deep. He was lucky not to be knocked unconscious when his head hit the bottom. He quickly stood up, and his friends' laughter turned to screams when they saw the blood streaming from a cut on his forehead and from his nose.

The doctor at the game reserve's medical centre inspected Karl's nose, said it did not look broken and simply gave him some painkillers. Despite his unease and pain, Karl trusted the doctor's advice and tried to enjoy the remainder of the holiday.

After returning home a few days later, Karl looked in the mirror to find that his nose had collapsed. He rushed to hospital and was seen by an ear, nose and throat (ENT) specialist, an elderly gentleman, who immediately recognised Karl's surname. The specialist recounted how, as a junior at medical school, he was put through a year-long rite of passage – an initiation process involving uncomfortable challenges and rituals – by Karl's grandfather, who was a medical school senior at the time.

Inspecting the X-rays, the ENT specialist – an expert with many years of experience – pointed out a fracture high up on Karl's nose and said that he would have to operate. Worried about scarring, Karl wondered about a possible incision. The specialist assured Karl that he would operate via his nostrils – one reason that ENT specialists are known as the watchmakers of the medical industry.

Early the next morning, as Karl lay waiting nervously on the operating table, with the bright theatre lights shining in his eyes, the anaesthetist placed the gas mask over Karl's mouth and nose. Just before he dozed off, the ENT specialist said, 'Now I am going to get you back for everything your grandfather did to me in medical school.' Before he could respond, Karl was out.

About two weeks after the operation, Karl was amazed by the results. The specialist had not only repaired the fracture, but he had also removed a life-long bump in Karl's nose. A few weeks later Karl discovered that the intermittent nosebleeds he had always struggled with had stopped entirely. The watchmaker ENT specialist had not only fixed Karl's nose – he had fixed his latent defects too!

Karl often wonders if the game reserve doctor was even qualified. Perhaps he was a wildlife veterinarian standing in for the doctor. The best word we could find to describe the game reserve doctor is *spuddling*, from the word *spuddle*, which means to work hard but achieve nothing.[1] Although the word is dated and seldom used, we find it also accurately describes the efforts of many data analytics leaders today.

Why did Karl believe the spuddling doctor's diagnosis without question? Karl realised many years later it was because he had been young and naïve and certainly not medically savvy. Despite his unease, he lacked the confidence, based on his knowledge at the time, to challenge the doctor's advice. It was only after his nose collapsed that Karl sought expert advice.

The watchmaker ENT specialist easily identified a fracture by looking at the X-rays, something that was well beyond Karl's abilities, who could not see the fracture on the X-rays even when it was pointed out to him by the specialist.

We include this story to illustrate the general challenge and opportunity for data analytics in companies. Building the right knowledge and confidence in the data analytics journey and identifying and involving the right experts can turn initial failures into significant successes, without you waiting for your investments to collapse.

Hype has led business leaders to believe that data analytics is a non-negotiable to survive and thrive. However, many companies have tried but failed to create any real value through data analytics. Business leaders consequently lose confidence in their ability to harness the power of data analytics to drive value. If you find yourself in a similar position, this book is for you.

There is a stark contrast within the world of data analytics. On the one hand, you have likely been bombarded with the success stories of top companies leveraging data to drive remarkable results. On the other hand, research shows that, globally, four out of five data analytics projects fail[2] – a reality we have witnessed. Whether due to high experimentation or poor planning and execution, the fact is that investments in data analytics are not yielding the desired results.

This paradox creates an exciting yet frustrating landscape. Many business leaders face challenges with unlocking data analytics value due to a lack of clear methodologies, limited experience, and a market of data analytics skills that are still developing the maturity required to generate and sustain real value.

Do you feel unsure about how to fully leverage data analytics for value creation?

Are you being held back by a lack of confidence in applying data analytics to generate value?

If the terms *decision paralysis* or *inability to commit* resonate with you, it may be worth reflecting on whether a lack of confidence is holding your company back in an area that requires brazen confidence to succeed. If you feel disorientated in a data-driven world, inertia may be preventing you from driving valuable results with data.

How do you overcome these hurdles?

Shortly after we met in 2022, we (Karl and Zjaén) realised our shared passion for addressing this challenge. Together, we have nearly forty years of experience in driving results with data, and we have each been called on by some of the world's largest companies to help transform their data analytics journeys. Our similar conclusions led us to write this book, consolidating our approaches into a powerful, actionable methodology.

Our objective is to enable you to become a data-confident leader. Imagine the impact you could have if you were the catalyst that spearheaded the achievement of exciting data analytics-driven results for your company. You can achieve this by applying the frameworks we will share with you. Within these pages, you will find secrets and strategies the top performers have painstakingly discovered to unlock their data value. These insights will enable you to overcome inertia and accelerate your data analytics journey.

While this book delves into some complex concepts, it is designed to empower you. We will explore new territory and uncover how companies drive value through data. We will focus not on the technical details but on how business leaders can drive data analytics-led *value*.

> Engage fully with the content and revisit the material as needed to reinforce the concepts. To further support your journey, we have made additional resources available on our website: **rappidvaluecycle.com**

You may have been intimidated in the past by technical people overcomplicating matters, but with the right guidance, becoming data value-savvy is within your reach. See this book as an intelligence augmentation that will enable you to go toe to toe in any technical discussion as you draw the focus away from the mundane towards the most vital component: driving valuable results. Progress in this area is key to remaining relevant as a business leader and vital for your company's growth, so approach the content with determination.

We have experienced a few failures ourselves over the years, but they only fuelled our determination to develop a robust methodology that ensures success. There are no formally accepted approaches and methodologies related to the universal challenge of extracting value through data analytics. This opens the door to varying and often weak opinions, each seemingly solving the whole problem but in reality focusing only on a specific symptom.

Through extensive collaboration with our multidisciplinary teams, we identified and overcame the factors that hindered success. Many companies have achieved substantial cost savings and revenue growth by implementing our methodology. Examples can be found at **rappidvaluecycle.com.**

Inspired by these results, we decided to publish this methodology. The chapters of this book offer frameworks for mastering value delivery through data analytics and overcoming strategic challenges.

In Part One we discuss how you can become a catalyst for identifying opportunities to drive value through data analytics. We then discuss how you can use the RAPPID Value Cycle – a comprehensive approach containing a proven set of frameworks – to confidently navigate the data analytics journey.

In Part Two we cover the full scope of the various RAPPID frameworks, starting with recognising value and succeeding at investing in insights. Next we discuss building a world-class data analytics function with a strong data value culture, defining a winning approach to delivering insights, and establishing a cost-optimised data platform. Lastly, we show you how to ensure that data analytics-based insights can be trusted for decision-making.

This book's third and final part introduces a new paradigm for data analytics-driven success, uncovering our Data Value Assurance framework. We explain how the data value architect applies the principles in this framework to bridge the gap between the competing priorities of cross-functional leaders and teams, ensuring the successful realisation of value from data analytics-led initiatives.

The challenges of the data analytics-driven world are vast but so are the opportunities. This book equips you with the confidence and frameworks needed to drive success, avoiding the pitfalls of trial and error.

It would be beneficial to start your journey by completing our Driving Results from Data Scorecard to assess your current capabilities and identify areas for growth. This scorecard is a valuable starting point and takes only a few minutes to complete. You can access it here: **rappidvaluecycle.com/drivingresults**

This book will guide you to becoming a data-confident leader capable of driving unparalleled value through data analytics. We are confident that, with the insights and strategies provided, you will be well equipped to lead your company to new heights, while propelling your personal value proposition forward.

> The diagrams in this book can be downloaded from the book website: **rappidvaluecycle.com**

A NOTE FOR DIVISIONAL AND SUBSIDIARY LEADERS

The concepts in this book are designed to help you make a significant impact within your area of responsibility, even if you lead at a divisional or subsidiary level in a group of companies. You may face shared corporate service constraints. The strategies and methodologies will empower you, despite your constraints, to influence your data analytics journey.

The frameworks in this book are flexible and scalable, enabling you to adapt them to your division's specific objectives. Success in data analytics often requires collaboration across different functions, and this book contains frameworks for establishing strong formalised relationships with other leaders in your company to drive a unified approach to data analytics value creation. Additionally, the frameworks will help you optimise the use of available technology resources and experts from shared corporate services, ensuring cost-effective and strategically aligned data analytics-led initiatives.

Applying the concepts discussed will directly impact key business outcomes within your division such as revenue growth and operational efficiency.

A NOTE FOR CDAOs

If you are a chief data and analytics officer (CDAO) or any other type of data analytics leader, you might find that the content in this book is not tailored specifically to your role. However, this book bridges the gap between you and your CxO counterparts. It will build their data-confidence, enabling them to better collaborate with you on data analytics-led initiatives.

While this book provides frameworks you might already be familiar with, its primary goal is to elevate business leaders by improving their understanding of and commitment to data analytics. Helping your CxO peers become more data value-savvy will make it easier for you to secure the necessary support, funding and alignment needed to drive value through data analytics-led initiatives.

Reading this book will benefit you due to its focus on value. Read it and share it with your CxO counterparts. Their improved data-confidence and ability to interact more positively around data analytics concepts will support your efforts to deliver value for your company. You can drive greater business growth and transformation as a unified leadership team.

The applied meaning of data analytics

Our use of the term *data analytics* in this book includes all forms of data analytics, from basic business intelligence driven by spreadsheets through to advanced techniques such as statistical analysis, machine learning or AI. In our definition of *data analytics*, we also include the sub-disciplines required to enable data analytics, like data engineering, data consolidation, etc. Regardless of the method used to generate it, all data analytics has the same objective: providing insights that have the potential to generate value.

Limitations of the RAPPID Value Cycle

While the RAPPID Value Cycle offers guidance for generating value through data analytics-led initiatives, it is important to recognise certain limitations. This book does not provide step-by-step practical implementation details. These are covered in additional consultative processes and online resources.

While advice is given on managing stakeholder buy-in, the nuanced intricacies of this process may require further consideration. The RAPPID Value Cycle assumes a relatively sound business operating model. Without this foundation, some recommendations may not apply.

Finally, the application of the methodology may face resistance from certain C-suite executives, particularly those who are highly risk-averse or resistant to change, which could limit the value you can realise.

PART ONE

THE FOUNDATIONS FOR GENERATING AND SUSTAINING DATA ANALYTICS-LED GROWTH

ONE

Paving The Way To Data Analytics-Driven Value

This book differs from many others on data analytics. It is not about producing actionable insights. It is about how to propel your business into a phase of accelerated growth, just as some of the companies we will mention were able to achieve.

The most recent research we could find on the success rates of data analytics projects is a 2018 Gartner report.[3] This report predicted that by 2022, only 20% of data analytics projects (one in five) would generate value. Our recent observations indicate that success rates have declined as more companies experiment – and fail to generate value – with data analytics-led initiatives.

Global spending on big data and analytics was projected to reach $350 billion in 2024, which means that an estimated $280 billion of investments made in 2024 likely yielded no value.[4] Your company might have contributed to this statistic.

High failure rates stifle innovation

As few as 13% of data analytics projects make it into production, and even fewer realise any value.[5] These statistics are skewed negatively due to a recent increase in experimentation with data analytics projects.

Rather than focusing on the exact failure rate, we are more concerned that opportunities are being missed. Leaders become more risk-averse when projects fail, and as a result, innovation is stifled.

This book equips you with the tools needed to increase your success rate, which will fuel your drive to innovate.

The root cause of high failure rates is twofold:

1. Like the spuddling doctor in the story in our introduction, many data analytics leaders still need to develop the skills to focus data analytics-led initiatives on value creation, i.e. beyond simply producing actionable insights. They work tirelessly yet are unable to produce any meaningful results.

2. To justify their contributions and cover up their shortcomings, data analytics leaders intimidate business stakeholders with conversations about technical details in an attempt to justify their misaligned contributions and cover up their shortcomings. As a business leader, you might feel like a naïve patient receiving a suspicious diagnosis, unsure how to challenge your data analytics leaders, despite your discomfort.

Together, these two factors risk the collapse of your company's investments in data analytics-led initiatives.

Our objective with this book is to equip you, as a business leader, with the knowledge and confidence to help your company progress boldly on a data analytics journey.

Business leaders can bridge the gap

The reason for projects failing does not always lie with the data analytics leader. Many data analytics leaders are hindered by business leaders who are not data value-savvy. These data analytics leaders struggle to get the necessary funding and support because their stakeholders do not have the knowledge or data value expertise to invest confidently in data analytics-led initiatives, and because these stakeholders often oversimplify the efforts required to realise

value. This lack of confidence and commitment contributes to wasted investments.

With the current hype around AI, it is essential to note
that creating value from AI is highly unlikely if your
company is not already generating value through
data analytics. We once presented the opportunity for
a manufacturing company to have immediate access
to information about the attendance of their workforce of thousands. The idea was to predict the attendance behaviour of team members so that supervisors
could know who would potentially be off sick the
next day, thereby enabling planning adjustments to
limit the impact on productivity. The client's response
was priceless: 'Why would we want to see who will
be at work tomorrow when we cannot even see who
should be at work today?'

Think of it as needing to crawl before you walk – research
shows that companies that skip levels only contribute
to the wasted investment statistic. AI's potential for
value generation is built on a solid foundation of data
analytics capabilities, and there is no magical shortcut
to circumvent this, no matter what hype your software
vendors would like you to believe. This book focuses on
establishing the foundations for driving value through
data analytics, ensuring your company is ready for
more advanced AI applications in the future.

Improving the data-confidence of business leaders is crucial to ensuring that investments in data

analytics and AI initiatives deliver the expected value. Ultimately, the responsibility for success lies with you as a business leader, and this book will provide you with the knowledge you need to grab this responsibility with both hands to drive valuable results.

CASE STUDY: Google versus Yahoo

Consider the story of Google and Yahoo during the early 2000s. Both had access to vast amounts of user- and platform-usage data.

Google recognised the potential of this data and, despite the risks, invested heavily in data analytics to drive value.[6] The insights enabled Google to continually enhance its search algorithms, improve advertising efficiency, and develop new products like Google Maps and Gmail. As a result, Google experienced exponential growth and became a dominant force in the industry.

On the other hand, Yahoo struggled with inconsistent strategies, a lack of focus, frequent leadership changes and shifts in strategic direction, all of which led to confusion and missed opportunities to capitalise on its data assets.[7] These factors contributed to Yahoo losing ground to Google.

In 2016 Verizon bought Yahoo for $4.83 billion,[8] which was 0.9% of Google's market cap at the time ($539 billion).[9] At the time of writing, Alphabet Inc. – Google's holding company – boasts a market cap of around $2 trillion.[10]

Brett StClair, previously Google's Head of Products for Africa, Greece and Israel, shared with us that every decision made at Google is critiqued based on the data backing that decision, whether that is for funding allocations, project approvals or organisational structuring. Data-confidence and data analytics-driven value are high on the priority list for all senior leaders at Google, not just for the data analytics leaders. Google made data their business – a strategy that has helped to propel them into the trillion-dollar market cap club.

Does anyone even care where Yahoo is now? The case of Google vs Yahoo is a stark reminder that companies that were once great are quickly forgotten when their competitors win the dog fight. Don't let this fate befall your company. Your competitors are leveraging data to generate value. It's best to get in the ring or risk defeat.

At the time of writing, seven of the top ten companies by market cap worldwide are data-first companies – either tech companies or outright data companies.[11] Market cap is not the only way to measure a company's value, but it gives a good idea of the perceived value. Top companies that are data-first are succeeding in generating value. We would not be surprised to see all top ten spots occupied by data-first companies in the next few years.

Note: Please do not take this as investment advice.

The data analytics challenge

Many companies are using data like a rockstar wields an electric guitar, playing personalised customer experience solos that are so good they top the charts. Meanwhile, others are stuck with a dusty old gramophone churning out the same old product and service tunes.

The data revolution is here, and those who fail to act will fall behind. Companies leveraging data are growing exponentially, while those that do not are lagging. The chasm between leaders and laggards is widening.

On which side of the chasm do you find yourself?

Are you a leader or a laggard, or are you actively trying to traverse the chasm while the voice in your head keeps reminding you not to look down?

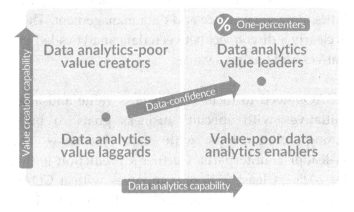

The quadrants of data analytics laggards and leaders

Your company has immense opportunities to generate value from data analytics, but as a business leader, you must become data-confident to identify and seize these opportunities. You will be surprised at how much value you can uncover when you know where to look.

Top-performing companies – the *one-percenters* – combine data value-savvy business leaders with watchmaker data analytics leaders, increasing EBITDA by up to 25%.[12] What portion of the potential 25% EBITDA uplift are you capitalising on?

But many of the front-runners are facing challenges. The NewVantage Partners '2023 Data and Analytics Leadership Executive Survey' highlights that only 4.8% of chief data officers (CDOs) and chief data and analytics officers (CDAOs) focus primarily on business use cases.[13] The rest prioritise data strategy, analytics, data governance and data management. There is clearly a disconnect between data analytics-led initiatives and business value.

CDAOs need to focus on business value and align initiatives with specific business goals to build strong relationships with their business- and IT-leader counterparts. Gartner's prediction is that by 2025, at least 25% of companies with a CDAO with business-orientated KPIs and reporting lines into business functions will likely achieve significantly higher market valuations than those without those elements.[14] This is exactly what Gartner says it is: a prediction. However, looking back at successful prior predictions released by Gartner, this one is believable.

CDAOs often focus on data governance and privacy, which tend to gain more support – thanks to shared interests in risk management and compliance – from their CxO counterparts (with CxO referring to various executive-level positions, including CEO, CFO, COO and CMO, among others). However, many CDAOs struggle to generate measurable value through data analytics because of challenges working with their CxO colleagues – substantial effort is required to achieve cross-functional alignment of priorities and objectives. CDAOs require defined methodologies and frameworks to manage this complexity and to drive data analytics-led collaborations with CxOs.

This book bridges that gap, providing business and IT leaders with the knowledge to build their data-confidence. It will develop your understanding of the process of delivering value through data analytics, and it will enable a unified approach to drive your company's bottom line. In the same way your brain develops new neural pathways when you form new habits, forming new data analytics habits and processes, for better communication and collaboration across your leadership team, will naturally improve your ability to drive value.

Working closely with your leadership counterparts is essential for driving value. Appointing a data value-savvy executive committee gives a massive advantage in generating value, and this is a critical tactic used by the one-percenters. This is far more productive than expecting your CDAO/CDO to fight a solitary battle. We recommend reading this book as a team to enhance your alignment. Value manifests through the collective *we*. Data is everyone's business.

The reality of achieving success with data analytics

Generating sustainable value from data analytics is often over-romanticised. The excitement of experiencing initial value is quickly overshadowed by the need for the foundational capabilities required to sustain that value, and that need is often considered too burdensome. Without strong foundations, though, the complexities of sustaining value will eventually surpass your capabilities, and the value will be lost.

The rest of this chapter explores this delicate balance, illustrating through historical parallels and modern examples how companies can achieve remarkable value while facing significant challenges to sustain it. It explores the fine balance of the data analytics journey, revealing the truth behind creating sustained value.

CASE STUDY: Foundational structures support success

In the late nineteenth century the idea of building a canal in Panama to connect the Atlantic and Pacific oceans intrigued engineers. The canal had to cut through 80 kilometres of land.

Ferdinand de Lesseps, the French mastermind behind the successful construction of the Suez Canal, attempted the ambitious Panama Canal project in the 1880s. However, this initial attempt failed due to a combination of technical challenges, financial mismanagement and the devastating impact of tropical diseases.

The United States took over the project in the early twentieth century. President Theodore Roosevelt saw the Panama Canal as essential to furthering the strategic and economic interests of the USA, as it would facilitate quicker maritime passage between the west and east coasts. He appointed Lieutenant Colonel George Washington Goethals to lead the project. At the time the project was considered one of the most noteworthy engineering challenges in the world.

From the outset, Goethals faced severe challenges, including a harsh tropical climate, torrential downpours, dense jungle terrain, treacherous landslides, and the spread of deadly illnesses among the canal workers. All these factors made excavation and construction extremely challenging and threatened to render the project a failure.

One of the most challenging aspects was managing the water flow and raising and lowering ships to enable their passage through the canal. With a land elevation of about 26 metres to contend with, a series of massive locks had to be built. It required an outstanding feat of engineering prowess.

Goethals, understanding the importance of a healthy workforce, implemented strict disease control and sanitation measures that were much more stringent than COVID-19 protocols. These foundational disciplines ensured that construction could proceed efficiently.

Despite having to deal with the same challenges faced by the French, Goethals and his team overcame the obstacles by implementing the necessary risk mitigation initiatives. They thought creatively to build innovative solutions and did not let any difficulty defeat them, despite continuously facing severe challenges.

The Panama Canal was a historic achievement that revolutionised global trade, with 40% of US container traffic – around $270 billion in value – now passing through it annually.[15]

The success of the Panama Canal project serves as a testament to what can be achieved, with solid foundations and innovative solutions, despite immense challenges.

With the high failure rate of data analytics projects, companies face major challenges in generating value through data analytics-led initiatives. These obstacles can feel as daunting as building the Panama Canal, especially for large companies with low data-confidence and legacy mindsets, where projects cost millions and can take years.

Unlocking sustainable value through data analytics differs greatly from what the marketing hype would have you believe. It requires deploying solutions across multiple complex business and IT processes and functions in unison. Additionally, companies are under immense pressure to innovate and stay relevant. Managing all this complexity while facing a divide between CDAOs, business leaders and IT leaders contributes to the high failure rates of data analytics projects.

Overlooking key foundations threatens value realisation

As companies grapple with the challenges of generating sustainable value using data analytics, companies renowned for their technological dexterity have faced their own rather costly data-related setbacks.

CASE STUDY: The cost of neglecting data foundations – a catastrophic failure

NASA is renowned for its use of data, achieving many feats that have changed the trajectory of innovation. However, even with top engineering minds on board, they are not immune to data issues causing catastrophic loss of value.

In 1999 NASA lost the $125 million Mars Orbiter due to a measurement system error.[16] An external team used imperial measurements, while NASA engineers used the metric system, leading to incorrect navigational information.

After 286 days of travel, the probe fired its engine to enter Mars orbit but with incorrect thrust, causing it to enter an unsuitable orbit about 25 kilometres

too low. The propulsion system overheated, causing
the spacecraft to leave orbit. It is now assumed to be
somewhere in the solar system, orbiting the sun.

This story is a stark reminder that missing foundational data management processes can have a catastrophic impact. Without the right foundations, failure
in data analytics is likely and can often be spectacular.

The world of tech and data is fraught with peril. Four
of the largest companies, all data analytics-led, cut
almost 60,000 jobs in 2023 alone, with Microsoft cutting 10,000 jobs, Google cutting 12,000, Meta cutting
10,000 and Amazon cutting 27,000.[17] These references
showcase the global impact of technology evolution
on leading companies. If data-first companies are facing these challenges, we can only imagine the difficulties that lie ahead for those that are struggling to drive
results from data. Even Apple, a company renowned
for its resilience and minimal layoffs since 1999, has
not been immune to the recent upheavals, while Intel
and Cisco are also reducing their workforces substantially.[18] These disruptions signal a significant shift in
the industry, highlighting the necessity for companies
to adapt and find new revenue streams.

In such a volatile environment, building robust data
analytics foundations is not just about avoiding
cost-cutting decisions. It is about ensuring your company remains competitive and resilient in an increasingly uncertain future.

Why companies struggle to drive data analytics-led value

Companies find it challenging to become data-driven, but therein lies the problem. Considering data analytics as a hammer, there is a tendency to see every business problem as a nail. Pursuing the objective of becoming data-driven reinforces the idea that data analytics is crucial for every scenario, regardless of the value it will produce. This places weak data analytics business cases above the usual scrutiny from business leaders, leading to the approval of projects based largely on intuition and an attempt to drive the misdirected data-driven agenda. But as the statistics show, these projects are doomed from the start.

Consider the youngest child – born years after their next youngest sibling – often receiving privileges the older children did not usually receive because the parents are older and more relaxed and have more disposable income. Similarly, data-driven initiatives often receive special privileges to get approval, causing a hype-driven misdirection of energy for solving all things data. Value remains a distant afterthought.

This hype-driven mindset causes shareholders to pressure boards to grow value quickly through data analytics. However, the journey takes time, and moving too quickly leads to failure. The contradiction that strong foundations are necessary for success, but value must be shown while building foundations, explains why companies find this journey challenging.

Legacy companies operating with traditional business models are relatively rigid and often deal with conservative people and legacy processes and systems. This prevents them from adjusting to new ways of working and delays their ability to pivot to new opportunities. They invest in data analytics in an attempt to become data-driven, trying to emulate global leaders who have scalability and agility built into their foundations. But the rigidity of legacy companies prevents them from adjusting to new ways of working and delays their ability to pivot to new opportunities.

Companies are often driven by hype or a fear of missing out (FOMO). Technology implementations incorrectly become the Holy Grail for success. It is easy, even for seasoned executives, to get caught up in technology hype, as marketers and salespeople innovate their messaging. Value must be the primary consideration when investing in new technology that is aligned with the company's strategic objectives.

Companies embark on massive IoT (Internet-of-Things) initiatives, leading to unmanageable volumes and complex data requiring resources that cost more than the value they create. They want to measure everything that moves in a misguided attempt to be data-driven, but this on its own does not produce value. There is sense in this quote: 'Data is like garbage. You'd better know what you are going to do with it before you collect it.'

Instead of being data-driven with value as a secondary consideration, aim to be value-driven and enabled by data. This mindset switch, which can be brought about by becoming data-confident, solves many challenges.

With the high failure rate of data analytics projects, it is understandable that many companies fear investing in this area. However, a cautious approach risks failure, making it crucial to build the confidence to unlock investments. This book provides the tools to help you do just that.

Driving value from data analytics must become part of your company's DNA. The narrative must change from *We might be successful* to *We cannot afford to fail* – the big-game mentality adopted by great sporting teams. This mindset ignites urgency and intention. Appointing a CDAO and hoping they will solve this alone will not work. Your entire leadership team must be aligned and motivated to succeed.

The stakes are high on a data analytics journey, and the road is challenging, as with Goethals and the Panama Canal. You need a measured approach to avoid failure and embarrassment. Consider and mitigate the risks. Your team needs discipline and frameworks. By addressing these foundational elements, your company can avoid similar pitfalls and confidently pursue data analytics-driven initiatives.

Generating and sustaining value with data analytics

Success in data analytics requires more than just implementing fancy tools. You need solid foundations that will outlast technology changes. This requires three pillars:

1. Value

2. Acceleration

3. Confidence

It is important to generate value quickly to build momentum, while avoiding intermittent failures that will slow you down. Simultaneously, you must build foundations to sustain the value. You will need to start with identifying the right opportunities to generate value from data analytics, and this book will show you several frameworks to build foundations for sustaining value.

Identifying opportunities to generate value from data analytics

For many, data analytics means readily available information in the form of reports and dashboards, which is a low-value starting point. Value from data analytics can be greatly increased by integrating results into business processes and business applications, enabling more employees to take value-generating actions. Tracking the actions taken and measuring and publishing the value generated is as important as the insights themselves.

Reports and dashboards typically generate indeterminate value, which is tangible but impractical to measure, making it difficult to justify ongoing investments. In contrast, determinate value – being tangible and easily measurable – provides more confidence in the results generated from data analytics-led initiatives, creating momentum for further investment. We expand on determinate and indeterminate value with examples in Chapter Three.

To succeed in generating substantial value through data analytics, you need to:

1. Identify opportunities to generate determinate (measurable) value and motivate for investment

2. Execute initiatives to leverage those opportunities producing trusted and valuable insights

3. Apply insights to business processes and business applications

4. Recognise the value generated to motivate for further investment

Most companies have generic opportunities to generate value from data analytics, which we will explain in the following sections, with examples that illustrate how you can potentially move the dial for your company. Identifying and capitalising on these opportunities can transform your company. By leveraging data analytics, you can drive growth and innovation.

Maximising revenue by addressing revenue leakage

Companies with complex billing rules driving subscription revenue will likely face uncertainty in revenue collection. Mobile networks and pay TV providers typically face this challenge, as do several industries such as utilities, telecommunications and software as a service (SaaS). We have previously built solutions that have identified millions of dollars of revenue leakage due to incorrectly applied billing rules.

Once a company identifies revenue leakage through data analytics, corrections can be made to billing rules, systems, and processes to align with revenue agreements, enabling leaked revenue to be collected. Automated revenue assurance analysis can then be rerun regularly to identify ongoing revenue leakage, especially when changes are made to complex billing rules, or after launching new products. This recovery of revenue can add substantially to the bottom line as you are effectively collecting revenue at a higher margin because the company already has entitlement to the revenue, without having to incur customer acquisition and delivery costs in earning it.

Revenue assurance is a good starting point for data analytics because it drives the top line, produces easily measurable value and creates success stories that build leadership confidence. This, in turn, drives stakeholder confidence and unlocks more investment in data analytics-led initiatives.

Growing revenue through cross-sell or upsell initiatives

We have seen significant success in companies that track and analyse detailed customer spending behaviour. By enhancing their data with third-party sources, they can determine effective levers for presenting cross-sell and upsell offers with a high probability of conversion.

We have successfully leveraged product and buying patterns and real-time customer segmentation for online retailers, presenting real-time cross-sell and upsell opportunities. For instance, customers browsing golf clubs might also be interested in golf balls. You have a small window of opportunity within which to offer them something of value – the *window of maximum value*. If you miss that window, the potential revenue gain is lost.

Online retailers typically place a section on their websites, called *Customers who looked at this product were also interested in these other products*. However, you may have found that these recommendations seem more random on some websites than on, for example, the leading online retailers. This is usually due to limitations in the data models driving these recommendations and leads to missed opportunities and lost value. Successful implementation of cross-sell and upsell initiatives requires robust data analytics solutions and supportive business processes to operate in real time, driving revenue growth.

Companies outside e-commerce can also benefit from cross-sell and upsell initiatives. By analysing data, patterns emerge that can inform new product packages, special offers and personalised interactions, all of which could lead to additional revenue.

Growing revenue through data analytics-driven marketing

Many companies use several social media and other platforms for their marketing campaigns. These platforms become valuable yet disparate data sources, delaying the analysis of consolidated marketing information. Challenges are also faced when integrating other data sources, like customer purchase behaviour from internal sources, or third-party external data sources. Incomplete data can result in producing below-target lead quality and conversion rates, leading to overspending on campaigns.

Our experience shows that near-real-time marketing insights based on complete and diverse consolidated datasets allow faster refinement of audience segmentation, quickly identifying segments that yield the highest returns from marketing spend and ultimately generating better-quality leads and more revenue.

Growing revenue by improving existing products

Your customers are hungry for new product features that will meet their needs. Adding data analytics or AI-driven product features to enhance an existing product can enable you to:

- Collect more revenue from a new product feature

- Make the product more competitive

- Extend the product's lifetime value

Software platforms incorporate AI to create improved product features that accelerate specific processes and enhance their value proposition. For instance, a fleet and logistics company uses AI-driven machine-learning models to optimise their roadside assistance services. The models accurately predict the required spare parts and skillsets, ensuring optimal stock levels and timely service. Additionally, the analysis ensures that

41

the right mechanical engineering skills are available in the right areas with optimised travel time, so customer wait times are reduced. This improves the product's value proposition and enables the company to charge more while remaining competitive.

Growing revenue by introducing new products

Adding new products using data analytics or AI can create new revenue streams for your company. For example, lifestyle companies have successfully incorporated health, insurance, fitness and entertainment features into their products. Data from existing products helps them identify how to influence the adoption of new products.

Rewards programmes leveraging data analytics influence the quicker adoption of new products. For instance, customers may be rewarded for swiping a pharmacy rewards card at participating fuel stations, with loyalty rewards influencing their buying behaviour.

Protecting revenue by predicting customer churn

Customer loyalty increases long-term revenue. However, in competitive markets, achieving loyalty is challenging. Customers often switch brands for better prices or service, or for easier sign-up processes.

Accurately predicting customer churn allows for proactive revenue-protection strategies. For example, customers on fixed mobile data contracts may exceed their limits, incurring high charges, which prompts them to switch providers. Identifying churn patterns enables timely interventions to retain customers by offering alternative solutions, within the window of maximum value.

Optimising costs and processes with data analytics

The previous sections all focused on revenue growth and protection. Focusing first on revenue growth and protection is often more impactful, especially in revenue-driven industries like SaaS, media and entertainment, and digital products. Companies that operate in a revenue-driven industry can yield substantially more value by focusing on revenue-generating initiatives, versus spending the same effort on cost-saving initiatives. The principle in play here is that *you can't save your way to greatness.*

Cost-saving is incorrectly seen as a data analytics priority in many companies in revenue-driven industries, driven by CFOs that lack data-confidence and therefore limited knowledge of how to focus on data analytics-led revenue growth opportunities instead. Don't get us wrong – costs need to be managed, but when companies throttle necessary expenditure due to ignorance of potential value, revenue growth opportunities are lost.

Having said that, data analytics can uncover significant cost-saving and process optimisation opportunities in companies that operate in cost-driven,
capital-intensive industries like manufacturing,
where profitability improvements are often driven
by internal process optimisation. Revenue growth
through diversifying their products usually requires
large capital-intensive initiatives like expanding manufacturing capabilities or acquiring companies.

In one example of a data analytics-led process optimisation and cost-saving initiative, a client of ours, a
manufacturing company, suspected significant over-
time abuse among its 10,000 employees. A data analytics solution confirmed the overspend of several
million dollars annually and identified the root cause.
With the right insights, processes were improved
and managers could address the issues, reducing
the wastage.

Another client of ours considered investing in technology infrastructure upgrades due to process bottlenecks suspected to be caused by ageing technology.
Data analytics identified the true root causes, which
were not technology-related, but were instead found
to be system issues that caused unexpected downtime, with the relevant fixes being applied during
standard operating hours instead of after hours, further exasperating the matter. IT managers were repri-
manded, and process changes were made, eliminating

bottlenecks and saving millions in unnecessary investment in new technology.

There are many ways to generate value through data analytics. However, please take note that cost-saving initiatives often require highly accurate, granular data, while also demanding substantial resources and platform investments. This can make it difficult to justify required investments which makes unlocking value challenging and costly, pointing to revenue uplift as a more viable initial focus.

Driving value with data analytics: The evolving role of the C-suite

The data analytics journey often begins with the CEO asking the CFO to 'unpack the numbers'. While data analytics is typically adopted with a focus on cost saving, many companies soon realise the potential of data analytics in revenue generation. Some have even formed entire businesses around earning revenue by providing data to a specific industry such as companies that provide third-party datasets to the retail industry.

Including data analytics in revenue-generating activities can also be out of necessity, based on a company's business model or industry. For example, real-time fraud analytics is necessary for banks and fintechs to manage risk.

Many companies that want to generate value from data analytics have appointed a chief data officer (CDO) or chief data and analytics officer (CDAO). A newer title – chief data and artificial intelligence officer (CDAIO) – is emerging due to the growing importance of AI. There is also an emerging trend that points to data science being called *cognitive science,* which will likely open the door for the role of chief cognitive science officer.

The data analytics function, headed up by any of these CDAO-type roles, is established and operates like an IT department for data analytics, usually requiring supporting disciplines like data engineering, data architecture and data governance. The data analytics function must focus on driving value through data analytics for business use cases.

A partnership between the CFO and the data analytics function (CDAO) is crucial for success. A Gartner study suggests that by 2026, CDAOs who become trusted advisers to CFOs will elevate data analytics as a strategic growth driver.[19] Pay close attention to this prediction. We have already started seeing a trend of value creation in many of our clients due to bridging the gap between CFOs and CDAOs.

This partnership has the potential to become a strong value-creation team if two factors are in place:

1. The CFO must be able to invest confidently in data analytics-led initiatives through strong justification by the CDAO.

2. The CDAO must be accountable to the CFO, proactively recognising and reporting on the value generated.

   This positive cycle of confident investments and measurable returns produces a value-driving partnership. We call this the *RAPPID Value Cycle*.

Both leaders need to develop an appreciation for the other's area. CDAOs must develop the ability to support their CFOs' requirement for confidence in investing, and CFOs need to build the data-confidence required for productive collaboration with CDAOs. It is not only up to the CFO, though. Each C-level executive has opportunities to leverage data analytics for value in their area, from growing revenue to optimising processes and reducing costs. We have heard several C-level executives blame their CFO for failing to invest enough in the data analytics capabilities required to meet the ever-growing needs of the company.

Whether you are a CFO or any other C-level executive, you must take accountability for developing business cases for your area of responsibility to justify investments in data analytics-led initiatives and capabilities, and then collaborate with your CDAO to pitch for investment to turn those ideas into value.

These are the secrets of the one-percenters that have propelled their companies to become leaders in driving data analytics-led value. They prioritise data-confidence in appointing their C-suite because they understand how to generate value with data, and the individual priorities of the C-suite concerning data analytics-led initiatives align with those of the CFO and the CDAO.

Strategic focus areas for each C-level

Value for any C-level executive comes from delivering on their objectives and key results (OKRs) or key performance indicators (KPIs). For the CHRO, it might be successful talent management. For the COO, it might be customer retention. The following diagram shows high-level priorities for each C-level executive that data analytics can support, and it can be used as a quick reference guide to identify potential focus areas for data analytics-led initiatives.

We have included a limited number of C-level roles in the diagram. For more detail, refer to the diagrams on the book's website: **rappidvaluecycle.com**

Keep in mind that key focus areas for all C-level executives will be alignment with the overall business strategy, efficiency and return on investment (ROI).

CIO
- IT ROI
- IT cost-to-revenue ratio
- IT risk management
- IT performance and efficiency

COO
- Revenue growth
- Profit margin
- Working capital management
- Operational efficiency

CRO
- Revenue growth
- Sales efficiency
- ROI for sales
- Sales pipeline management
- Sales growth

CMO
- Marketing ROI
- Marketing performance and efficiency
- Customer experience and brand

CDiO
- Digital revenue growth
- Digital product/service performance
- Innovation
- Cost optimisation

CFO
- Financial performance
- Cash flow management
- Cost management
- Financial risk management

CEO

- Strategic vision and leadership
- Risk management
- Growth and financial performance
- Innovation and adaptability
- Stakeholder management

Focus areas for the C-suite

Final thoughts on building data analytics-led value

People have always sought faster travel. As cargo needs grew, trains were invented, but some people still focused on breeding faster horses – they could not imagine any other solution. They were stuck in the *We have always done it this way* mindset. Ultimately, their lack of resourcefulness and inability to think differently caused them to miss many opportunities.

These seven words – *We have always done it this way* – represent the biggest hindrance to innovation and value creation. Generating value from data analytics requires new thinking, different from what made companies successful twenty years ago. Consider whether this mindset is holding your company back.

Remember, the path to generating and sustaining value from data analytics is not easy, but it is immensely rewarding. See your challenges as opportunities to transform your company, through growth and innovation. Embrace these challenges with a mindset of resilience and curiosity.

You have made some good progress already. You should now be well-versed in how to identify – or at least commission the identification of – several value-generating initiatives (VGIs) that can be enabled by data analytics.

In the upcoming chapters, you will find practical frameworks and strategies to help you build strong foundations to sustain value. The journey may be challenging, but you will succeed if you stay committed – the destination is well worth it. The next chapter will kick off your RAPPID data analytics journey.

Key chapter takeaways

- Increasing business leaders' data-confidence is crucial to the success of data analytics-led initiatives.

- History has shown that strong foundations increase the probability of success. Generating sustainable value from data analytics requires strong foundational capabilities, as initial value generated diminishes without them.

- The goal of data analytics-led initiatives should be value-driven and enabled by data analytics, not merely data-driven. This shift in mindset reduces high failure rates and leads to more robust business cases.

- Business leaders need to avoid the traps of moving too quickly, especially with technology implementations, succumbing to FOMO and failing to focus on value. Instead, they must prioritise value and establish solid foundations for long-term success.

- The partnership between the CDAO and CFO is critical for maintaining a cycle of consistent investment and value realisation from data analytics-led initiatives. Successful data analytics efforts require alignment and collaboration across the entire C-suite, with each executive responsible for driving value in their respective areas.

- Value-generating initiatives focused on revenue growth usually achieve better results than cost-saving initiatives and are therefore better as an initial focus for data analytics.

A NOTE FOR DIVISIONAL AND SUBSIDIARY LEADERS

Your division may face the typical challenges highlighted in this chapter such as misaligning data analytics-led initiatives with business value, overlooking foundational requirements, and reacting to hype or FOMO-driven trends. Your challenges may differ from those of the rest of the group, or they could be similar.

To ensure success, focus on aligning your projects with strategic goals; building strong data foundations; and maintaining a disciplined, value-driven approach to technology adoption. Identify opportunities to generate value through targeted initiatives like revenue assurance, customer churn analytics, and enhancing customer experiences.

By prioritising value-driven outcomes and avoiding common pitfalls, your division can contribute substantially to your group's overall success.

TWO

Navigate Your Data Analytics Journey RAPPID-ly

A major battle faced by many companies on their data analytics journey is the inevitable winds of change that can so easily derail progress. You may often feel like you are taking one step forward and two steps back. Strong foundational structures enable easy adaptation to change, whether in response to opportunity or risk.

Strategic planning: The key to data analytics success

The following story highlights how crucial planning and strong foundations are to the data analytics journey.

CASE STUDY: Transforming the data analytics function to drive value

A few years ago, we worked with a client in the SaaS industry, who had been wrestling with a persistent challenge. Despite their efforts, they battled to drive strategic growth through data analytics-led initiatives. They felt exasperated, unable to unlock the potential hidden within their data.

Recognising the critical importance of data in their growth strategy, the client turned to us for guidance. We stepped in to help them transform their data analytics function to drive value.

Over nine months, we worked closely with the client to build a team of data analysts, data engineers and project managers. We not only addressed their immediate problems but also focused on creating solid foundations that would support long-term growth and innovation and improve their ability to withstand inevitable business change.

As the client's data analytics journey matured, cost pressures forced an evaluation of their data platform. To reduce costs, they decided to migrate their entire data platform to a new cloud provider. This type of migration is one of the biggest challenges on any data analytics journey. The expectations were that this would be a painful and time-consuming endeavour, with significant risks of delays and disruptions. However, with the robust foundations we had established together, the client was well prepared to withstand the winds of change. What was initially estimated to take nine months was accomplished in just three, all within budget and with minimal disruption. The results were extraordinary: cloud data platform costs plummeted by 50% in the first month and decreased by 74% over the next four years. They not only met their objectives but surpassed them by a wide margin.

This agility enabled the client to accelerate their growth unhindered and included access to the latest data platform technology. Their new foundations enabled the client to overcome one of the biggest challenges on a data analytics journey, instead using it as a catalyst to seize opportunities for continuous growth and innovation.

You cannot operate in organised chaos while expecting success. Strong foundations distinguish those geared for success from those that are not.

In this chapter we will introduce you to the structures and concepts that enabled these types of successes so that you can apply the principles to your environment and start seeing tremendous improvements for your company. Before that, though, we are going to take you on a journey.

The data analytics journey

Most companies follow a typical data analytics journey, and we do not use the term *journey* lightly. You need:

- A clear understanding of where you currently are

- A vision of where you want to be

- Proper planning to know what is needed to get you there

The following diagram depicts the stages of this journey.

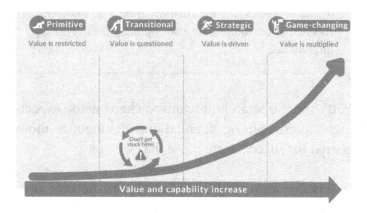

The four stages of the data analytics journey

1. The primitive stage

Most companies begin their data analytics journey in the *primitive stage*, characterised by spreadsheet-based reporting and with manual analysis performed mainly by the finance function and other pseudo-analysts across the business. Many companies find comfort in the rows and columns they became accustomed to in the late 1990s, and they still see no need to change. But the world has moved on.

In the primitive stage, rudimentary and outdated skills drive the narrative. As a result, developing analytics is time-consuming, with delays in obtaining valuable insights leading to decisions based on gut feel. Generating measurable value through data analytics-led initiatives is not even a fleeting thought.

These companies unknowingly lose ground to their competitors as they focus on maintaining operations. They have no capacity for optimisation or data analytics-driven growth. This restricts value.

The primitive stage is not limited to small companies. If this describes your company, do not fret. This book will help you justify investments in your data analytics journey to enable progress beyond the primitive stage.

2. The transitional stage

The *transitional stage* begins when a company establishes a formalised data analytics team of more than two professionals, which may include data scientists, analysts and engineers, and possibly project managers or data governance specialists.

In the transitional stage:

- Defined structures are lacking, and confidence in the team's delivery is limited.

- High maintenance effort limits capacity to innovate, and the team focuses primarily on building reports and dashboards.

- Business impact is constrained, and the value of delivery is questioned.

- Stakeholder discussions revolve around costs rather than value.

If the focus remains on cost for long enough, any data analytics function will be lined up to walk the plank, regardless of how specialised it is. Leaders chalk up the loss of the data analytics function as a casualty of doing business. But the root cause is never addressed, destroying trust and widening the divide between data analytics teams and business leaders, placing value in question.

If you are stuck in this stage, do not fret – this book will guide you to the *strategic stage*.

3. The strategic stage

Moving from the transitional stage to the *strategic stage* requires the establishment of foundations to enable consistency and predictable timelines for delivery. In this stage, robust planning and resource allocation allow the team to focus on building innovative solutions that align with the company's strategy.

In the strategic stage:

- The value of the team's delivery is measured and published, reassuring stakeholders that investments in data analytics yield valuable returns.

- Delivery has moved beyond reports and dashboards, focusing on integrating insights into business processes. This enables more employees to take decisive action based on reliable data.

- The one-percenters come into their own. They place value at the forefront of everything they do with data analytics, and they confidently make substantial investments in the required capabilities.

- The data analytics function becomes integral to value creation in the company, making it indispensable to driving value.

The story of our SaaS industry client at the beginning of the chapter is an example of a data analytics function that established the foundations required to move into the strategic stage. The frameworks in this book will enable you to do the same.

4. The game-changing stage

The *game-changing stage* is reached after moving through the strategic stage. Here companies use data creatively and innovatively, increasing their competitive advantage, becoming leaders in their industry, and sometimes creating new industries. Think of companies like Uber, Google, Amazon, X and Airbnb, and others that leverage data as a strategic differentiator that enables their core business.

In the game-changing stage:

- Data analytics is part of the fabric of the company, driving significant revenue.

- Integrated analytics solutions are woven into the company's innovative products.

- Innovation is a routine activity, with stakeholders being directly involved in actively planning future innovations for value generation.

- Collaborative teams from business, IT and data analytics functions work together to produce valuable data analytics-led products.

- There is a strong alignment with the business strategy, making data analytics a core value driver.

- Insights are provided both internally for decision-making and externally as products and services.

- Data analytics is essential to the company's operations.

In the game-changing stage, value is multiplied.

With the right conditions, your company could move into the game-changing stage.

This book focuses primarily on helping companies reach the strategic stage. While the foundational principles and frameworks outlined can also support the journey towards the game-changing stage, this book is not for the one-percenters looking to take this leap. In these pages we seek to elevate the knowledge of the other 99% and grow your data-confidence, so that you too can leverage the opportunities available in the lucrative world of value-driving data analytics.

Navigating through the stages RAPPID-ly

To move from the primitive stage into the transitional stage, a strategic mandate is required for the data analytics journey, largely due to the substantial investment required. We will explore how to obtain this strategic mandate in the following chapters by introducing you to the RAPPID Value Cycle.

The key to sustaining value from data analytics is to move through the transitional stage quickly, as remaining there is demanding and costly. Arguments about costs, together with continuously seeking value justification, erode trust and waste time and money. Investing to get through this stage quickly is worthwhile because the cost of staying there longer is higher than the investment needed to progress to the strategic stage. It is a lack of data-confidence that prevents leaders from making these investments as they struggle to identify the valuable returns they can achieve by moving to the strategic stage.

As a result, many companies get stuck in the transitional stage for years, which spirals them into a value drain. The team's delivery is constantly questioned, and discussions are focused on costs instead of value. Low stakeholder confidence makes for an unfulfilling work environment, so staff turnover is high, leading to a loss of institutional knowledge and expertise and an inability to build momentum. Eventually, the cost drain causes stakeholders to question the value of continuing the data analytics journey. Experienced data professionals have generally found a career in data challenging because they have spent too many years in companies stuck in this regressive spiral.

Foundational frameworks are required to bring structure to the team's delivery and to demonstrate value, to stop this regressive cycle, moving the company from the transitional stage to the strategic stage. This keeps stakeholders engaged, unlocks further investment and generates more value, creating a positive feedback loop.

In the rest of this book, we will show you how the RAPPID Value Cycle helps you progress through the transitional stage and on to the strategic stage in record time, avoiding the pitfalls where most get stuck. The RAPPID Value Cycle enables an exponential growth curve that accelerates as you progress through the stages.

Moving from the strategic stage to the game-changing stage, where value is multiplied, requires:

- The company's leadership team having strong data-confidence

- The right strategy, products, people and market conditions

- A high appetite for risk

- Substantial investment

Only a select few traditional companies, like Goldman Sachs, Freeport-McMoRan and Levi Strauss, have operated in the game-changing stage and seen exponential value growth.

Due to their data-first strategies, some of the most disruptive new businesses start their journey in the game-changing stage. These businesses often use

multi-sided platform business models to build sharing economy solutions, focusing on collaborative consumption and resource sharing, which require robust
data analytics. Examples include accommodation
sharing (Airbnb), ride sharing (Uber), peer-to-peer
lending (Prosper), and food sharing (Too Good To Go).
As mentioned before, moving into the game-changing
stage requires specific strategies and detailed guidance that fall beyond the scope of this book.

Now that you understand the stages of the journey,
we will introduce the components of the RAPPID
Value Cycle. Then we will guide you in diagnosing
which stage you are in on your data analytics journey, though you may already know from reading this
far. You must know your point of departure to know
what to focus on to improve. Based on this, we will
recommend how to consume the rest of this book to
optimise the value you receive.

Introduction to the RAPPID Value Cycle

This is not an academic exercise. The RAPPID Value
Cycle is grounded in practical experience, placing
value at the core of data analytics. It draws on decades
of working with companies and data leaders across
various industries and regions. The methodology
offers a comprehensive solution by addressing real-life
challenges and removing barriers to value creation.

The RAPPID Value Cycle helps business leaders to become data-confident without needing technical expertise. Benefits include:

- Accelerating the identification of value-generating opportunities

- Guiding value forecasting for investment pitches

- Enabling strong oversight for guiding data analytics-led initiatives to deliver value

- Understanding how to measure, publish and sustain value, enabling a positive cycle of continued investment in data analytics-led initiatives, leading to further value creation

In the 1960s, Harold Leavitt's People, Process, Technology framework illustrated the interplay between these three components and their impact on companies, and how change affects companies.[20] Over time the consulting industry integrated *data* as the missing element connecting people, processes and technology.

The RAPPID Value Cycle extends the People, Process, Technology framework for the end-to-end data analytics journey by including *recognising value, investing* and *data*.

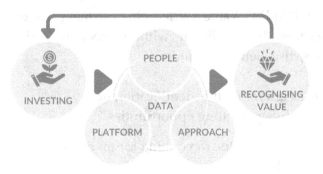

*The RAPPID Value Cycle, related to the People, Process,
Technology framework*

Each RAPPID component is supported by a framework that helps business leaders focus on key concepts to accelerate value in their data analytics journey, as shown in the diagram below.

In addition to studying the diagram below, we recommend downloading the RAPPID Value Cycle diagram from the book's website, and printing it in large format. Use it to record notes and insights as you read this book. There are many connections between the nodes of the methodology, and the RAPPID Value Cycle diagram prescribes a flow that is fundamental for driving a successful data analytics journey.

> The RAPPID Value Cycle diagram is available at
> **rappidvaluecycle.com/diagram.**

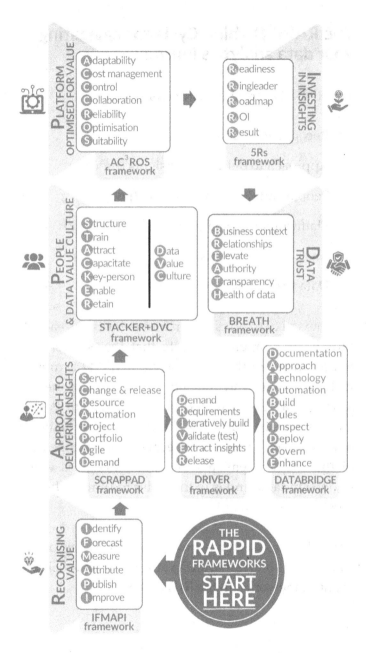

The RAPPID Value Cycle and associated frameworks

The RAPPID Value Cycle for navigating your data analytics journey

The RAPPID acronym stands for:

- Recognising value

- Approach to delivering insights (process)

- People and data value culture (people)

- Platform optimised for value (technology)

- Investing in insights

- Data trust (data)

The next six chapters cover frameworks for each of the above components. Note that the chapters are not arranged in the order of the RAPPID acronym. If the acronym were spelled in the order of the following chapters, it would be RIPAPD, with People and data value culture as the first 'P' and Platform optimised for value as the second. The arrangement of the chapters ensures the methodology is easily understandable and is in the order recommended for most readers.

The following sections provide an overview of the components of the RAPPID Value Cycle and their relevant frameworks, in the RIPAPD order.

Recognising value: The IFMAPI framework

This is the starting point for any successful data analytics journey. Recognising value from potential solutions will address many challenges that would keep you stuck in the transitional stage, and it will enable confident ongoing investment.

Why do we start with *recognising value* if that is at the end of the value chain of the RAPPID Value Cycle? To succeed with generating value through data analytics, you first need to understand how you are going to recognise value. You must begin with the end in mind.

The IFMAPI framework, covered in Chapter Three, offers a proven approach to identifying value-generating initiatives, forecasting their potential value and building the capabilities to measure the value generated. It also enables the attribution of value generated to the relevant business functions that contributed, publishing the value in a format that engages stakeholders, and routinely monitoring to improve value generation.

Implementing the IFMAPI framework will transform a data analytics function to a value-driving profit centre rather than it being viewed as a cost centre. This shift will yield numerous benefits, including changing stakeholders' mindset from cost-focused to value-focused.

Chapter One highlighted the importance of the CDAO and CFO relationship in elevating data analytics as a strategic value driver. The IFMAPI framework is the first major connecting point between the CDAO and CFO, providing a foundational structure for this relationship.

Investing in insights: The 5Rs framework

Funding is a fundamental requirement for driving value through data analytics. However, funding alone will not sustain value once your environment crosses a threshold of complexity. At that point, you risk losing all the value you have generated. Therefore, funding must also be allocated to building the foundations required to advance from the transitional stage to the strategic stage, which will sustain the value generated. Convincing your CFO to make the substantial investments required to build these foundations is key to success.

This is the second major connection point that brings the CDAO and CFO together as a powerful team to elevate data analytics as a strategic value driver.

In Chapter Four we will present a foolproof method to pitch for investment in a data analytics journey using the 5Rs framework, significantly improving your chances of securing the necessary funding and continuing to receive funding as you progress.

People and data value culture:
The STACKER+DVC framework

People and culture are your most important success factors on a data analytics journey. Your ability to attract, grow and retain strong data professionals is fundamental to generating value. Understanding the nuances of managing data professionals will help you overcome the skills shortage by enabling you to become an employer of choice as data professionals seek opportunities to be involved in cutting-edge initiatives.

In Chapter Five you will discover how to apply the principles from the STACKER+DVC framework to build your data analytics function as a world-class team while establishing a strong data value culture.

Approach to delivering valuable
insights: The SCRAPPAD, DRIVER and
DATABRIDGE frameworks

The ability to maintain focus is an important characteristic of companies in the strategic stage. A structured approach to delivering valuable insights enables robust stakeholder expectation management to vastly accelerate delivery timelines by keeping the team focused on critical priorities.

A data analytics function involves many moving parts. Delivery management, data analytics delivery, data architecture and data engineering must all collaborate to produce valuable outputs. The SCRAPPAD, DRIVER and DATABRIDGE frameworks explored in Chapter Six will ensure your data analytics function runs like a well-conducted orchestra, freeing the capacity to build innovative solutions that will enhance the impact and value of their delivery.

Platform optimised for value: The AC³ROS framework

In data analytics the only feeling worse than getting the wrong data on time is getting the correct data too late. Knowing how to select and optimise data platforms to generate returns on investments will vastly accelerate your journey. Poor platform choices often plague companies in the transitional stage, wasting money on failed implementations and migrations.

The AC³ROS framework, to be explored in Chapter Seven, offers a non-technical, solid foundation for data platforms and technology implementations focused on driving value.

Data trust: The BREATH framework

Frustrations with unreliable data and endless debates over business definitions and data rules hinder decision-making and progress on the journey.

The BREATH framework, to be explored in Chapter Eight, eliminates doubts about data sources, calculations and analytics results by guiding you to publish important information alongside your data analytics and insights to make them more reliable, which enables confident decision-making, driving more value.

Now that you have a brief overview of each of the frameworks of the RAPPID Value Cycle, we will guide you on how to effectively use the methodology to maximise value based on your point of departure.

Maximising value with the RAPPID Value Cycle

As the first step in maximising value, we will help you determine your current stage in the data analytics journey.

Which data analytics journey stage are you in?

To determine your current stage, you can reflect on your company's journey to assess whether you are in the primitive, transitional, strategic or game-changing stage. Knowing your stage will help you navigate the rest of this book effectively.

If your company relies heavily on spreadsheet analytics and lacks a dedicated data analytics function, you are likely in the primitive stage. Additionally, you may be in this stage if any of the following apply:

- You lack a published strategy or clear roadmap for a data analytics journey.

- You have a strategic mandate or roadmap but have not yet started the journey.

- You have a very small team (fewer than three people) that has started the journey.

- You have attempted only one or two data analytics projects.

You are in the transitional stage if you have a formalised data analytics function with three or more people, but you are not producing recognised value consistently yet, and data analytics is not yet seen as a core business enabler.

You are in the strategic stage if your data analytics function produces recognised value and receives investment and focus from stakeholders as a core business enabler, supporting key strategic objectives directly.

To confirm the assessment of your stage, we have a Journey Stage Evaluator that takes only a few minutes to complete. Access it here: **rappidvaluecycle.com/journeystage**

Now that you know which stage you are in, we will recommend an approach for reading the rest of this book.

Primitive stage: Recommended approach

While starting from the primitive stage might feel daunting, remember that every data analytics-driven success story begins here. With the right approach, you can transform your company's analytics capabilities and unlock tremendous value.

In this stage, you will likely face challenges when taking the first steps on a data analytics journey to the transitional stage. You might need help identifying opportunities to generate value through data analytics. You may already have tried pitching for investment in a data analytics journey or project and realised your plan had gaps or had this pointed out during a presentation.

Do not be discouraged if you feel unsupported by your leadership team in starting a data analytics journey. We have found that most pitches for data analytics journeys or projects lack strong motivation for approval. This is one of the reasons we created the RAPPID Value Cycle – to help you pitch successfully next time, improving your ability to impact your company positively. Chapter Four will show you how to prepare to pitch successfully.

Pitch essentials: Are you pre-strategy or do you already have a strategic mandate?

There are two categories in the primitive stage. You are either pre-strategy, or you have a strategic mandate already issued (with or without funding).

Before you pitch, it is essential to know whether you already have a strategic mandate for formalised data analytics. This will help you know where to start and what to focus on.

A published strategic mandate typically looks like a formal instruction from your board or company head, directing you or another leader to embark on a data analytics journey. Sometimes the instruction might be less clear, such as repeated verbal requests to *Do something about the fact that we cannot see what is going on in our business!* A budget or funding might have been allocated along with the strategic mandate, but this is not always the case.

If you are pre-strategy, we recommend first obtaining a strategic mandate and funding. Without this, you cannot start a formalised data analytics journey to move from the primitive to the transitional stage. We will explain how to obtain a strategic mandate and funding in ten defined steps in Chapters Three and Four.

If you have a strategic mandate but no assigned funding, focus on Chapter Four to develop a roadmap and

ROI model, including a budget, to pitch for funding and expenditure approval.

If you already have a strategic mandate and funding allocated, read Chapters Three and Four carefully, as you will still need to justify expenditure approval, which is not automatically guaranteed simply because you have an allocated budget. You still need a roadmap and an ROI model for expenditure approval to start your data analytics journey. Those two chapters will help you establish that expenditure plan to get approval.

A note for smaller companies

Note that smaller companies might struggle to kick off a formal data analytics journey. If your company generates less than $10 million in annual revenue, you might lack the necessary use cases or complexity to justify a formal data analytics journey.

Generating less than $10 million in revenue doesn't mean you can't do analytics. It just means that a for-malised data analytics function might not be feasible due to the challenge of justifying the investments. In this case, for more basic analytics requirements you can use in-application analytics functionality.

For more complex requirements where you need to consolidate data from various applications, prebuilt consolidation tools should satisfy your requirements.

These tools are readily available, especially for the more standardised business functions like marketing and finance. You will start facing challenges when initiatives require custom data consolidation and data analytics. In that case, outsourcing to a reputable consulting company on a project-by-project basis may be worthwhile, provided you can justify the investments by forecasting measurable returns.

Exceptions exist where smaller companies can justify substantial investments in a data analytics journey, such as when aiming to implement a revenue-generating data analytics solution with substantial returns forecasted. Another exception is the need for analytics due to regulatory or compliance requirements in some industries. In this case, company size and revenue may be irrelevant.

Transitional stage: Recommended approach

Being in the transitional stage means you can put in the effort now to position your company for sustainable success. Stay focused, and you will see the rewards of your dedication. Your objective is to create a plan to advance promptly to the strategic stage. Focus on specific chapters of this book, based on your journey and the challenges you face, to determine how to make quick improvements.

Remember that there is unfortunately no quick fix to reach the strategic stage. A well-structured programme of interconnected work across the various frameworks is essential to establish the necessary foundations.

Regardless of your journey stage, read Chapter Three. Recognising value is a fundamental discipline for a successful data analytics journey to build a positive value cycle.

Chapter Four is essential, as the journey to the strategic stage requires foundational investments in people, consulting and likely technology too. Before seeking additional funding from stakeholders, you need to be able to prove the value of potential results, which is another fundamental discipline in building a positive value cycle.

Strategic stage: Recommended approach

Reaching the strategic stage is a significant achievement. Your company already benefits from a value-producing data analytics function. Celebrate this success, while continuing to refine and innovate. Remember, your hard work has brought you here, and the journey only gets more rewarding.

However, there is always room for improvement, with the game-changing stage being a desirable target. We recommend working through Chapters Three to Eight in sequence, focusing on areas for improvement to reinforce your value cycle. Pay special attention to recognising value, as this is where many companies face roadblocks.

Final thoughts on navigating your data analytics journey

Navigating the data analytics journey is like learning to play a complex musical instrument. At first you might be stuck in the primitive stage, where every note is a struggle and progress is slow. With the right investment and guidance, you can move into the transitional stage, where you start to understand the basics and begin to see the potential of what you can achieve. Remember, enduring this phase is necessary despite the challenges and costs because it is part of the journey to immense growth.

Think of moving from the transitional stage to the strategic stage as moving from playing simple tunes to performing symphonies. Learning is no longer a frustrating burden as the satisfaction that comes from making progress creates a cycle of willing investment to keep improving. Here your data analytics value cycle becomes an integral part of your company, consistently attracting investment and growing its impact. With the right conditions and continuous improvement you can reach the game-changing stage, where your company not only leads the industry but sets new standards through innovative and creative use of data. You will be leading a world-class orchestra.

This chapter has highlighted the importance of strong foundations and structured approaches for success in your data analytics journey. Each stage presents unique challenges, but with perseverance and the right strategies, you can overcome and drive substantial value for your company. By introducing the RAPPID Value Cycle, we have begun laying the groundwork for understanding the critical components and frameworks necessary to advance effectively through each stage. Irrespective of how you choose to read the book and which sections you need to focus on most, we strongly recommend covering all the chapters, as there are interdependencies between the frameworks.

No matter where you are on your journey, you have the potential to achieve excellence in data analytics. As you proceed, remember that the path to data analytics-driven success is not linear but an exponential growth curve. Every challenge you overcome strengthens your foundations and brings you closer to leading your industry. Embrace the journey with a mindset of resilience and curiosity. Here's to your success in unlocking the full potential of data analytics.

Key chapter takeaways

- Strong foundational structures are essential for navigating the inevitable changes and challenges in a data analytics journey, enabling companies to adapt quickly and successfully.

- The data analytics journey consists of four stages – primitive, transitional, strategic and game-changing – each with its challenges and opportunities for value creation.

- Companies that progress to the strategic stage can achieve significant value, while those that reach the game-changing stage can lead their industries by using data as a strategic differentiator.

- Understanding your current stage is crucial to effectively navigating your data analytics journey and achieving success.

- Moving from the transitional stage to the strategic stage quickly is crucial for sustaining value, as remaining in the transitional stage leads to high costs, eroded trust, and wasted resources.

- Strategic investment and robust planning are required to reach the strategic stage, where innovative solutions are created and value is driven. This requires recognising value early in the data analytics journey to build trust to secure the required investments and justify the costs associated with advancing to the strategic stage.

- The RAPPID Value Cycle offers a practical, value-driven approach to progressing through the stages of the data analytics journey, focusing on building solid foundations and delivering measurable value.

A NOTE FOR DIVISIONAL AND SUBSIDIARY LEADERS

You may find that your division or subsidiary is at a different stage in the data analytics journey from that of the broader group. This is normal, especially with acquisitions. An investigation exercise may be required to identify where you are in relation to the group. It is crucial to tailor your approach to align with your specific stage and any corporate strategic mandates, identifying opportunities to synergise and leverage successes and valuable resources from across the group.

You may need to secure a strategic mandate, specific to your division, and obtain the required funding. You can leverage the RAPPID Value Cycle to build strong foundational structures, to ensure that your data analytics-led initiatives are both effective and aligned with the company's overall objectives.

Corporate resources can be used more effectively to drive value when you have built data-confidence in your division's leadership team.

PART TWO
THE RAPPID
VALUE CYCLE

THREE

Recognising Value – The IFMAPI Framework

Implementation of the IFMAPI framework will have a profound impact on your company. The systematic recognition of value generated from data analytics investments separates those companies that achieve great success with data analytics from those that languish in the doldrums of the transitional stage. The IFMAPI framework is one of the primary reasons we wrote this book. It can be the turning point for your company, guiding you towards remarkable success and growth.

Remember that we cover *recognising value* first because we are beginning with the end in mind. Succeeding with generating value through data analytics first requires you to understand how you are going to recognise value.

Chapter One highlighted the critical relationship between the CDAO and CFO in elevating data analytics to a strategic level. This relationship must be aligned to succeed on a data analytics journey. With limited alignment, you can expect only limited value. To fully realise potential value, strategic focus must be aligned, and two important intersection points must be established:

1. The CDAO must systematically report to the CFO on the value delivered.

2. The CFO must confidently justify investments in data analytics capabilities and initiatives to enable the CDAO to generate value.

The result is a healthy, value-generating collaboration that drives a positive value cycle.

The IFMAPI framework and the 5Rs framework (covered in Chapter Four) together establish the foundational structures that sustain the CDAO–CFO relationship. Either framework would be ineffective without the other – they operate in unison.

The first key intersection point between the CDAO and CFO enables the CFO to track the progress of value delivery, which is the purpose of the IFMAPI framework.

Overcoming the CDAO's challenge:
The impact on value creation

We regularly speak with CDAOs about their roles. One CDAO, who had been promoted through the ranks and consistently delivered value in previous roles, shared his growing frustration. Despite leading a team that developed innovative dashboards across business areas, he found himself in endless meetings, struggling to justify the necessary investment for the data analytics roadmap. Although expectations for delivery remained high, investment had dwindled, leaving him questioning his future with the company.

Unfortunately, this experience is common among CDAOs.

Replacing a CDAO is costly in terms of lost institutional knowledge, in the impact on investment confidence, and (most significantly) in opportunities missed because of tentative investing brought about by the lack of recognised value.

Reduced investment confidence stems from the absence of a clear, published view of the measurable value that data analytics-led initiatives generate and of their alignment with strategic objectives. Often the focus is on the wrong initiatives – like reports and dashboards – that don't deliver clear, measurable value, making decision-makers hesitant to allocate funding.

The real tragedy is that decision-makers withhold investments in lucrative data analytics-led initiatives often due only to a lack of clear information on past value generated and on the impact on strategic objectives. This halts the company's progress.

While this is common, it is also surmountable. The one-percenters have managed to align their leadership teams by bringing their collective focus to value recognition. With the right strategies you too can overcome these challenges and lead your company to greater success.

In this chapter we will introduce the foundational IFMAPI framework that places value recognition at the core of your data analytics efforts, enabling confident investment in high-impact initiatives. We will also introduce a powerful communication tool to keep value in clear focus, enabling continuous monitoring and improvement.

Before diving into the framework, we must cover two key concepts:

1. The economics of data and information

2. The classification of economic benefits from data analytics-led initiatives

A brief introduction to the economics of data and information

In our experience many data professionals face a fundamental challenge. They excel at 'speaking data' but often struggle with the language of the CFO – the language of *value*. It is important to understand that the CFO is a meticulously tuned machine, their eyes sharply focused on two main issues: risk and returns.

The CFO will likely have started their academic studies with an exploration of the definition of an asset according to the International Financial Reporting Standards (IFRS), and specifically the Conceptual Framework for Financial Reporting.[21] The definition is summarised as: 'A resource controlled by the entity as a result of past events and from which future economic benefits are expected to flow to the entity'.[22] In the CFO's mind, the value of data as an asset is directly related to the future economic benefits that can be coaxed out of your data through value-generating initiatives. Other than to serve this purpose, the CFO considers that data has no value.

If the previous paragraph felt a bit dense and you shut down as soon as you saw a quote from a financial reporting standard, try to reread it, but this time a little slower and in your best David Attenborough voice. That will help you get the important message from it.

Consider a property as an example of an asset. If the property is in a remote, uninhabitable location, its potential to generate economic benefit is low, and so is its value. Ultimately, the property's value is determined by the economic benefit a buyer expects to extract – your opinion of the value, as the property owner, makes no difference. The value of the asset is based purely on its ability to generate economic benefits.

Extracting value from data assets starts with identifying opportunities aligned with the company's objectives. Next it is important to forecast the economic benefits from these opportunities through actions that increase revenue, reduce costs and manage risk.

Why is strategic alignment and careful forecasting of value so important to data analytics-led initiatives? Simply put, a CFO would not invest in a property outside the company's objectives or without a forecasted positive return and manageable risk. The same logic applies to data analytics-led initiatives.

Finally, measuring, attributing and publishing the value generated by data analytics-led initiatives is crucial to proving the asset's worth. Without this, decision-makers will downplay the value of your data assets, and their enthusiasm for further investment will fade.

Classifying economic benefits from data analytics-led initiatives

Economic benefits (or value) – the returns CFOs focus on – are classified as tangible (measurable) or intangible (not measurable).

We take this classification one step further to improve how we identify, forecast and measure value, all of which are fundamental to aligning with the CFO's priorities. The key challenge we are addressing is that data analytics initiatives often produce tangible value that is difficult to measure accurately without excessive time and resources, making it economically unviable to do so.

EXAMPLE: Business performance dashboard

Consider a business performance dashboard showing financial metrics. The value it produces depends on:

- The decisions made based on the dashboard
- Its usage frequency (number of views)
- The cost, usually in person-hours, of producing the same information through other means
- The trustworthiness of insights from those alternatives and whether manual reconciliation is needed
- The cost of not producing the dashboard at all

> These components could be combined to produce the value generated by the dashboard. However, accurately measuring the dashboard's actual value would require complex statistical analysis, which would likely be more costly than building the dashboard itself.

We therefore categorise tangible value as:

- **Determinate value** – economically viable and easy to measure

- **Indeterminate value** – difficult and costly to measure, like the example above of the business performance dashboard

Several examples of producing determinate value from data analytics-led initiatives have already been provided in Chapter Two.

Intangible value remains defined as value that cannot be measured directly, with no further sub-categories in this framework. An example of intangible value is the overall improvement in employee morale when insights become accessible in the business processes for which they are responsible. They are happier and therefore perform better when they have access to the right data to make value-adding decisions. These benefits have lower importance than tangible benefits.

The transformative power of the IFMAPI framework

With a clear understanding of the fundamental concepts, let us now dive into the IFMAPI framework to explore how its components collaboratively support the recognition of value from data analytics-led initiatives.

The framework's six components are:

1. Identify value

2. Forecast value

3. Measure value

4. Attribute value

5. Publish value

6. Improve value

These form the acronym IFMAPI, as illustrated in the diagram below.

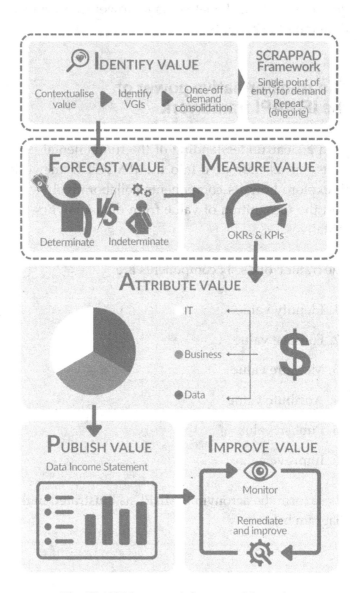

The IFMAPI framework for recognising value

We will now break down the components of the IFMAPI framework to show how they collectively support value recognition in data analytics-led initiatives.

1. Identify value

Identifying value varies from company to company. What drives success in your business may differ significantly from competitors, so defining value specifically for your company is crucial. This can be achieved by contextualising value, identifying value-generating initiatives through demand consolidation, and evaluating high-impact initiatives, as outlined below.

Contextualising value

Contextualising value means identifying what truly drives your company's success and focusing on that, starting with understanding your company's strategic priorities. This is not just helpful – it is essential. Contextualisation ensures all efforts align with your company's core goals. Without it, even sophisticated data analytics projects can waste resources and miss opportunities.

Failing to contextualise value isn't just a missed opportunity – it can harm your bottom line. Projects that don't align with your company's value drivers may lead to resource misallocation, lost stakeholder confidence and reduced ROI. Contextualisation protects against these risks.

Contextualisation also empowers leadership to make informed investment decisions. When value is linked to strategic objectives, decision-makers can allocate resources confidently, knowing their investments will yield measurable returns. Without this clarity, leadership may hesitate, slowing progress and reducing the impact of data analytics on growth.

Start by immersing yourself in your company's strategy. Review published documents like strategy papers, annual reports and board packs, and consult with senior stakeholders to understand their objectives and performance metrics. Examine past performance and research competitors to deepen your understanding.

Identifying value-generating initiatives (VGIs) through demand consolidation

With a clear understanding of value for your company, the next step is to identify use cases that will drive this value. We call these use cases *value-generating initiatives*.

It is crucial to note that identifying and then focusing on delivering high-value initiatives that can produce determinate (tangible) value will simplify the remaining steps in the IFMAPI framework – forecast, measure, attribute, publish and improve value. This approach will enable you to deliver results that build momentum, ensuring sustained investment and long-term value generation.

To assist you in identifying value-generating initiatives, the following is an example of a high-value use case with clear, measurable value. We will refer to this later in the book as *the call centre example.*

EXAMPLE: High-value use case in a call centre

This scenario typically occurs in a telecommunications company's call centre, where separate teams handle customer service and retention. If you held workshops with these managers, they might suggest improvements in customer retention as follows.

If customer service agents handling service requests know that a customer's contract is nearing its end, they could transfer the customer to the retentions team immediately after resolving the service issue and before ending the call. This would allow them to make a crucial revenue-protecting decision within the window of maximum value: deciding whether to transfer the customer to the retentions team while the customer is still on the line, potentially resulting in contract renewal.

This approach is preferable to the customer service agent ending the call without knowing the customer's renewal status. Missing this window of

---

opportunity means retention efforts have to rely on costly outbound retention calls with a lower chance of connecting with the customer, ultimately increasing the risk of losing revenue.

In this example, timely action – driven by placing the right insight in the right hands at the right time – can boost customer retention and, ultimately, company revenue.

Note that the valuable solution in this example did not require advanced analytics, machine learning or AI. The most valuable data analytics solutions are often the simplest, so don't limit your thinking by focusing only on cutting-edge solutions. Start with simple, valuable solutions to problems – they are usually the quickest to implement and yield the fastest results, building momentum for your journey.

Conduct a demand consolidation exercise to build a prioritised view of value-generating initiatives across your company. This involves gathering, stimulating and classifying business requirements from various stakeholders into a single repository. The process allows you to prioritise initiatives based on their expected value, significance to the company, and implementation and maintenance costs.

Some stakeholders may need help identifying high-value use cases. A demand stimulation exercise should be conducted with these stakeholders.

Identifying high-value use cases

Consider asking the following questions during demand stimulation workshops:

1. Are we confident that we are collecting all our contractually owed revenue? If not, how can we use data analytics to identify and address potential revenue leakage to maximise revenue?

2. How can we increase revenue by introducing innovative pricing models through data analytics, potentially increasing our margins?

3. How can we grow revenue by enhancing existing products or services with data analytics-driven features?

4. How can we expand revenue by launching new products or services through data analytics with existing or newly acquired data?

5. How can we leverage data analytics to identify customer segments likely to accept cross-sell or upsell offers on existing, improved or new products?

6. How can we apply our customer segmentation in data analytics-driven marketing campaigns to gain better and quicker insights and optimise for more and better-quality leads?

7. How can we safeguard revenue by using data analytics to predict and respond to potential customer churn?

8. How can we reduce costs by improving existing processes through data analytics?

This list of questions is non-exhaustive and can be expanded to include other value-generating opportunities such as regulatory compliance, risk management and enhancing customer experience.

To uncover further potential value, you can use divergent and convergent thinking techniques to identify additional questions posed in the form of 'How might we …?' For example:

- How might we increase our annual revenue?

- How might we increase our customer NPS?

- How might we produce better products?

If you expand these questions into areas with high-value potential, the answers can be unpacked to determine whether you can use data analytics to generate value. This exercise might expose process and system issues that can also be addressed.

Steps for effective demand consolidation

Comprehensive demand consolidation requires the following steps:

1. **Define the scope of demand gathering.** Identify and publish the level of demand (business

requirements) to be gathered. Narrow the focus to business requirements that align with strategic imperatives and that could generate determinate value.

2. **Gather demand.** Collect all business requirements or use cases from your stakeholders into a central repository.

3. **Stimulate demand.** Conduct workshops with stakeholders to identify value-generating opportunities in their areas of responsibility. Compile a list of valuable use cases during these sessions. See the suggestions for workshop questions mentioned previously.

4. **Clarify demand.** Gather additional relevant information such as business priority, demand owner, impacted business processes and required data elements. This helps build a detailed understanding of each demand item and informs follow-up planning and roadmap development (covered in Chapter Four).

5. **Align to strategy.** Link each demand item to the company's strategic objectives and value drivers (e.g., revenue growth, cost reduction, operational efficiency, sustainability).

6. **Classify value estimates.** Categorise each demand item's expected value into high-level buckets, noting whether the value is determinate or indeterminate. Identify intangible value too.

7. **Estimate implementation and maintenance costs.** Break down expected costs into high-level categories, separating expenses for people, consulting and technology. Remember that generating determinate value requires investments beyond only data analytics capabilities, such as integration with IT applications, changes to business processes, and employee training.

8. **Estimate delivery timeline.** Estimate the expected delivery timeline based on available information.

9. **Identify dependencies.** Track the dependency of demand items on the completion of other initiatives or projects.

10. **Prioritise demand.** Use a prioritisation matrix (effort vs. value vs. business priority) to propose the execution order.

A single point of entry for all demand

A one-off demand consolidation exercise as described above will help you build a consolidated demand list. Once completed, all new incoming demand should be processed through the SCRAPPAD framework in Chapter Six, which establishes a single point of entry for all demand. This is crucial to ensuring delivery is focused only on priority initiatives and for effectively managing stakeholder expectations. When implemented correctly, it eliminates the chaos often found in data analytics functions and greatly enhances their effectiveness and ability to deliver value.

The information gathered for each demand item through this single point of entry process is similar to the information gathered for the comprehensive demand consolidation explained earlier.

After completing a comprehensive demand consolidation exercise, a medium-sized company (200–500 employees) should have a list of approximately 50–100 demand items, with larger companies likely having more and smaller companies having fewer. This demand list should contain data analytics-led initiatives similar to the call centre example above, which will produce determinate value. It should not just be a list of KPI-tracking dashboards, which typically produce limited value because they describe what happened or what might happen, not what should happen.

When evaluating valuable use cases, it is essential to consider high-level cost estimates for implementation and maintenance. Use cases are valuable only if the expected value significantly exceeds implementation and maintenance costs.

Evaluating high-impact initiatives

Use this checklist for each high-priority initiative to ensure they are worth pursuing:

- Does this initiative support specific key strategic objectives?

- Will this initiative enhance the company's competitive edge?

- Are specific, measurable outcomes clearly forecasted?

- Do the expected costs align with the expected value for strong ROI potential?

- Is this initiative prioritised and aligned with the needs of key stakeholders?

- Will key business and IT stakeholders support the initiative?

By following this checklist, you will identify which initiatives will generate determinate value that is also contextualised.

Strategically stacking initiatives for investment justification

If your high-value initiatives have high implementation costs, don't worry – there is a way to manage this effectively. In Chapter Four we will guide you through a method to stack investments in your data analytics journey, allowing you to tackle valuable use cases that might initially seem cost prohibitive. It may sound unconventional, but it will make sense soon.

2. Forecast value

Forecasting value involves estimating the potential impact of your data analytics-led initiatives. This is important for two reasons:

1. To support a request for funding.

2. To have a forecast against which to benchmark actual value generated.

It is much easier to forecast the value of an initiative that will produce determinate value versus one that produces indeterminate value.

Forecasting determinate value

The call centre example demonstrates an initiative with potential to yield determinate value. Forecasting value here is far more straightforward than with the indeterminate value of a business performance dashboard. The forecasted value in the call centre example can be calculated as shown in the table below.

Item	Value
Average number of customers that are less than 30 days from their contract end date	100,000 customers
Average monthly revenue generated from customers that are less than 30 days from their contract end date	$50 per month per customer

Item	Value
Percentage of customers in the above category that place service request calls in the last month of their contract	5%
Average retention rate for customers where successful contact was made during the final 30 days of their contracts	50%
Revenue protection forecast (100,000 × $50 × 5% × 50%)	$125,000 per month

This straightforward forecast forms the basis of a strong business case and would stand up under the scrutiny of any competent investment committee. This ease of calculation highlights why it is preferable to pursue determinate value rather than indeterminate value.

If you are stuck with producing only indeterminate value

If your initiatives focus primarily on solutions like the business performance dashboard, where forecasting value is difficult, it is crucial to advance to initiatives with potential to produce determinate value. The next example shows how to extract determinate value from a dashboard typically associated with indeterminate value. It demonstrates how to convert dashboard insights into value-driving actions, the value of which can be measured. Adopting this approach will allow your forecast models to reflect more determinate value, even for dashboards.

EXAMPLE: The top-twenty customer dashboard

Suppose you have a dashboard listing your top twenty customers by revenue for the last month. On its own, this yields little value, but if you compare that list with the current month's top-twenty list, you can derive some insights. Investigate any 'drop-offs' to uncover why those customers are declining. These insights would be more valuable.

However, these insights must be converted to corresponding actions to generate determinate value. Value is questionable when actions cannot be derived from insights. For instance, if Customer A's revenue this month has dropped compared with last month, this 'fluffy insight' offers no actionable value without further investigation. At this stage, the value remains indeterminate.

If, on further investigation, you find that Customer A is facing financial difficulties that have led to reduced spending, you can recommend an alternative product or discounted pricing to prevent cancellation and the potential loss of the customer. This actionable insight can protect revenue, and you have unlocked potential to generate determinate value.

Extending this analysis over a longer period and across more customers could highlight the benefits of an automated solution when the results are shared with the appropriate stakeholders for the corresponding actions to be taken. Capturing and analysing the results of these actions is vital to

> improving the value and securing future investments in similar initiatives.
>
> Using value forecasting methods similar to those shown in the previous call centre example, a comprehensive financial forecast can be produced.

If you are limited to dashboarding and reporting projects, you still need to demonstrate value. Forecasting indeterminate value is more challenging than forecasting determinate value, but it is possible with some extra effort. This is where the *double Ds* come in – documented and defendable.

Forecasting indeterminate value

When you are forecasting value in situations where accurate measurements are difficult or economically unviable, make assumptions. The key to effective assumptions is ensuring they are well documented and defendable. Reasonable, documented assumptions are more likely to withstand scrutiny, thereby boosting stakeholder confidence in the forecasted value.

For instance, with the business performance dashboard example earlier in this chapter, an assumption model can be built to demonstrate that each view of the dashboard saves person hours, and therefore money, by avoiding manual report preparation. Additional value drivers might include the quick availability of information and the enhanced quality of data compared with a manually prepared report.

By applying an assumption model, these value drivers can be converted into a *value-generated-per-view* metric, for example, $50 per view of the dashboard. This approach is similar to the standard costing principle in manufacturing, which simplifies the allocation of complex costs to small units of production.

UNDERSTANDING THE STANDARD COSTING PRINCIPLE

The standard costing principle in manufacturing accounting assigns expected costs to forecasted production units, enabling companies to estimate manufacturing costs for large-scale production.

The principle involves forecasting standard costs for materials and labour, and for overheads such as property rental and electricity. These costs are then combined and divided by the forecasted production units to determine the standard manufacturing cost per unit. For example, if total raw material, labour and overhead costs for the year are expected to be $1 million, and the forecast is to produce a million units, the standard production cost per unit is $1.

> Standard costs serve as a benchmark for evaluating actual costs. A standard production cost is generated by multiplying the actual units produced by the standard unit cost. For example, in a specific month, if 80,000 units are produced, standard production cost is $80,000. This can then be compared with actual production costs to identify variances and address production issues.

When you multiply the number of dashboard views over a week or month by the value-generated-per-view metric of $50 from your assumption model, which is similar to the standard cost of a single unit of production, you can calculate the total cost saving for the dashboard for that period. If stakeholders approve your value-generated-per-view metric, and you can reliably estimate the forecasted number of dashboard views, you can forecast – and later measure – the indeterminate value generated by the dashboard.

3. Measure value

Measuring value is straightforward when dealing with determinate value because relevant data and calculations were already defined when forecasting, as seen in the call centre example. The same measurement criteria can easily be applied to measure the actual value generated. This again highlights the importance of focusing on initiatives with potential to produce determinate value.

It is important to consider that producing determinate value requires a collaborative approach that considers the entire data analytics value chain, not just individual components like a dashboard or data analytics capabilities.

Measuring indeterminate value

Measuring value is more challenging with the business performance dashboard due to the fact that it produces indeterminate value. However, using the assumption model previously created can provide a somewhat reliable view of the value generated. To do this:

- Extend the assumption model explained previously to measure indeterminate value, by multiplying the actual number of dashboard views by the value-generated-per-view metric.

- Use the same assumptions and metrics, as they should already have stakeholder approval.

- Ensure the calculations for the assumption model are published in a *value measurement* section alongside the dashboard, and that all assumptions are documented and defendable.

The uncertainty of these measurements further supports the case for focusing on initiatives that produce determinate value. When dealing with indeterminate value, consider translating them into determinate value by linking valuable insights to business processes that drive decisive actions, as illustrated in the top-twenty customers example above. In that case, you negate the need for an assumption model to measure indeterminate value, as the value is determinate.

Connect value measurement with OKRs and KPIs

Aligning your value measurement with company OKRs or KPIs will give leadership confidence, as this ties value creation directly into the company's primary performance indicators.

For example, link the call centre example to a KPI that tracks customer retention rates. This connection will engage stakeholders by highlighting the value generated from the data analytics-led initiative, elevating its profile and increasing support for similar initiatives.

4. Attribute value

The purpose of value attribution is to allocate value and recognition to the teams driving the success of data analytics-led initiatives. Data analytics functions are often seen as cost centres because the financial uplift they generate is credited to the relevant business division they are supporting. This perception limits investment in data analytics-led initiatives, hindering business growth and the company's potential to develop a competitive edge.

The value generated through data analytics-led initiatives often depends on complex, interlinked business processes. Without accurately matching generated value to the effort expended, business leaders may struggle to justify investment in the right functions, leaving high-potential initiatives untapped due to inaccurate information on sources of value generation.

In the call centre example, there are multiple contributors to the value generated:

- Data analytics teams build the data consolidation processes and insights.

- IT integrates insights into customer service applications.

- The customer service department adjusts processes and trains agents to use these insights.

This example highlights the collaborative effort required to generate determinate value with data analytics.

The value generated should be attributed based on the effort invested by each function, or in some cases, the data analytics function may claim the lion's share of the value due to its pivotal role in identifying and then developing the solution. Value attribution needs to be negotiated internally to reflect the agreed-upon contributions.

Value attribution is rooted in the idea that the whole is greater than the sum of its parts. By allocating the total value to individual processes and linking these to measurable KPIs across various functions, companies can clearly see each function's contribution. This transparency makes it very easy to identify bottlenecks and inefficiencies across complex, multifaceted and interdependent processes, enabling targeted remediation. The acceleration this brings to issue resolution can be astounding.

Record the value attribution agreement in a memorandum of understanding or in performance measurement documentation, signed by all parties, to ensure a shared understanding. As value attribution becomes wallet-impacting, written agreements will be essential to maintain decorum.

5. Publish value

We recommend the introduction of a powerful communication tool to highlight the value generated from data analytics-led initiatives, enhancing transparency of and accountability for value creation. This tool is our *Data Income Statement*.

The Data Income Statement consolidates the outputs of previous steps, including the identification, forecasting, measurement and attribution of value, and costs incurred to deliver data analytics-led initiatives. It combines these in a single report showing net value generated or lost. This transformative view positions the data analytics function as a profit-generating unit, which appeals to executives and decision-makers typically concerned with cost-based operations.

The diagram below shows an example of the Data Income Statement including the initial elements of this chapter: identify, forecast, measure and attribute (see the headings at the top of the dashboard). At a minimum, your data income statement should include:

- People, technology and consulting costs incurred

- Initiatives implemented

- Forecasted versus actual value generated

- Value attribution

The report can also include the intangible value from each initiative. These indirect value generators – such as employee growth and community upliftment – often complement the data analytics function's performance and may be valued by business leadership.

For more details on the Data Income Statement and for a downloadable version, visit this link: **rappidvaluecycle.com/dataincomestatement**

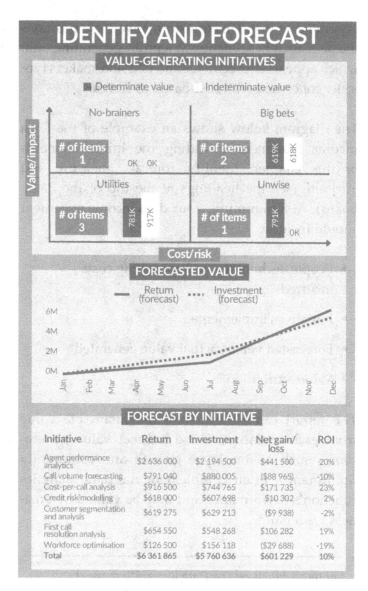

IDENTIFY AND FORECAST

VALUE-GENERATING INITIATIVES

■ Determinate value ☐ Indeterminate value

Value/impact

No-brainers	Big bets
# of items 1 0K 0K	# of items 2 619K 618K
Utilities	Unwise
# of items 3 781K 917K	# of items 1 791K 0K

Cost/risk

FORECASTED VALUE

—— Return (forecast)   ···· Investment (forecast)

6M

4M

2M

0M

Jan Feb Mar Apr May Jun Jul Aug Sep Oct Nov Dec

FORECAST BY INITIATIVE

Initiative	Return	Investment	Net gain/ loss	ROI
Agent performance analytics	$2 636 000	$2 194 500	$441 500	20%
Call volume forecasting	$791 040	$880 005	($88 965)	-10%
Cost-per-call analysis	$916 500	$744 765	$171 735	23%
Credit risk modelling	$618 000	$607 698	$10 302	2%
Customer segmentation and analysis	$619 275	$629 213	($9 938)	-2%
First call resolution analysis	$654 550	$548 268	$106 282	19%
Workforce optimisation	$126 500	$156 118	($29 688)	-19%
Total	$6 361 865	$5 760 636	$601 229	10%

The Data Income Statement

MEASURE AND ATTRIBUTE

VALUE ATTRIBUTION BY BUSINESS FUNCTION

■ Data function ■ IT Operations

Initiative			
First call resolution analysis	71K	47K	118.17K
Cost-per-call analysis	151K	38K	186K
Credit risk modelling	35K	35K	69.75K
Customer segmentation and a...	37K	25K	62.10K
Agent performance analytics	220K	24K	244K
Call volume forecasting	44K		63.36K
Workforce optimisation	22K		24.75K

ACTUAL VALUE

—— Return (actual) ····· Investment (actual)

6M
4M
2M
0M

Jan Feb Mar Apr May Jun Jul Aug Sep Oct Nov Dec

ACTUAL VALUE BY INITIATIVE

Initiative	Return	Investment	Net gain/ loss	ROI
Agent performance analytics	$2 518 200	$2 090 000	$428 200	20%
Call volume forecasting	$728 640	$838 100	($109 460)	-13%
Cost-per-call analysis	$885 600	$709 300	$176 300	25%
Credit risk modelling	$671 400	$578 760	$92 640	16%
Customer segmentation and analysis	$568 791	$599 250	($30 519)	-5%
First call resolution analysis	$592 020	$522 160	$69 860	13%
Workforce optimisation	$116 500	$149 750	($32 650)	-22%
Total	$6 080 691	$5 486 320	$594 371	11%

6. Improve value

The Data Income Statement should be used as a feedback tool to enhance the value generated by data analytics-led initiatives.

If the Data Income Statement reveals a significant gap between forecasted and actual value, it can spark crucial discussions that start with the question, *Why?* With accurate value attribution and relevant KPIs in place, you can quickly identify and address areas where value generation falls short, significantly accelerating remediation efforts. This work will tackle common issues that often hinder the success of data analytics solutions, such as poor data quality, change management and solution stability. Business process reengineering may be necessary to optimise underperforming value chain components.

Aligning performance reviews with accurate value measurements and assigning employee rewards according to the value generated will significantly improve results. This approach will help eliminate common challenges in data analytics, as your team will be motivated to address issues early in the development process. Implementing these changes may require negotiation, especially in highly unionised environments.

What is measured can now be managed. Value – the most critical component of any data analytics-led initiative – takes centre stage.

Key success factors for implementing the IFMAPI framework

Implementing the IFMAPI framework will significantly boost confidence in investing in data analytics-led initiatives. A structured process for identifying and forecasting value ensures focus on the most impactful initiatives. Consistent value measurement and attribution, and regular publication of value through a Data Income Statement, enhance accountability and reinforce value creation with continuous improvement.

Success factors also include:

- Aligning value recognition with business performance metrics

- Regularly training teams on the framework

- Incorporating value metrics in appraisals and incentives

- Periodically reviewing value measurements to match evolving business goals

Common pitfalls and how to avoid them

Common pitfalls include inaccurate value measurement and attribution, which can distort the published information on value generated. It is crucial to ensure data accuracy for making informed decisions on investments and incentives. Value measurement must align with company goals to ensure its relevance to stakeholders.

Resistance to continuous value recognition may arise as the company confronts areas of weakness. Be mindful of the impact of this change and provide adequate support and time for the necessary cultural shift. Increased transparency can lead to a culture of openness, honesty and accountability – a positive evolution.

Final thoughts on harnessing the power of value recognition

Think of the IFMAPI framework and the Data Income Statement combined as the compass guiding your data analytics journey, ensuring you are always on course to discover and extract real value. Just as the captain of a ship relies on instruments to steer through uncharted waters, your company can rely on this framework to chart a path towards success with data analytics.

The value recognition process is a transformative force that differentiates the companies that flourish on the journey from those that remain stuck in a swamp of unmeasured and indeterminate outcomes. The IFMAPI framework ensures that data analytics-led initiatives are closely aligned with strategic objectives so that measurable value is realised from investments.

The relationship between the CDAO and CFO is crucial in this transformation. Think of it as the partnership between the navigator and the ship's captain. The navigator (CDAO) provides the insights and direction, while the captain (CFO) ensures the resources are allocated and managed correctly to reach the destination. When the CDAO and CFO roles are aligned and operate within the structured processes of the IFMAPI framework, your company starts to shift from seeing data analytics as a cost to recognising it as a core value driver.

Now that you are equipped with the tools to recognise value, the next step is to secure investment for your data analytics journey. The following chapter introduces a framework designed to solidify the second crucial connection between the CDAO and CFO, arming you with a foolproof strategy to not only justify but also confidently secure the investments necessary for continued growth and success in your data analytics-led initiatives.

Remember that generating value from data analytics requires a continuous cycle of identifying, measuring and improving value to propel your company forward.

MAXIMISE YOUR RESULTS

If you are already generating measurable value through data analytics-led initiatives, improving your value recognition will accelerate your journey. Take the Results Maximiser Scorecard to find out where you can improve your value recognition.

Access the scorecard here:
rappidvaluecycle.com/resultsmaximiser

Key chapter takeaways

- The IFMAPI framework provides a structured approach to identifying, forecasting, measuring, attributing, publishing and improving value, ensuring that data analytics efforts are tightly aligned with strategic business objectives.

- Systematically recognising value from data analytics-led initiatives by implementing the IFMAPI framework is critical to moving from the transitional stage to achieving significant business growth and success with data analytics.

- Contextualising value by aligning data analytics-led initiatives with company strategy enables more confident and informed investment decisions, protecting against resource misallocation and ensuring high ROI.

- It is vital to focus on generating determinate (measurable) value to simplify value forecasting, measurement and attribution, ensuring sustained momentum and investment.

- The Data Income Statement is a powerful tool for communicating the value generated from data analytics-led initiatives, enhancing transparency and accountability, and demonstrating their profitability and impact.

- Continuous improvement in value generation is achieved by aligning value measurements with business performance metrics, regularly reviewing outcomes, and incentivising teams based on the value they generate, thereby fostering a culture of transparency and accountability.

- Collaboration between the CDAO and CFO is essential for securing investments and tracking value delivery, transforming data analytics from a cost centre into a core value driver for the company.

A NOTE FOR DIVISIONAL AND SUBSIDIARY LEADERS

As you implement the concepts from this chapter in your area of responsibility, consider the challenges you will face in contextualising and recognising value. The IFMAPI framework is powerful, but its success depends on how well it is adapted to your context.

The first step – identifying and contextualising value – requires you to align your data analytics-led initiatives with both corporate objectives and those of your division. This dual alignment is crucial to ensure that your initiatives resonate with corporate leadership, while also directly addressing your division's needs.

When it comes to value measurement and attribution, it is essential to ensure that your division's contributions are clearly recognised within the broader corporate structure. Your division should not be seen as a cost centre, but as a key driver of value. Given the limited resources often available at the divisional level, you need to prioritise initiatives that offer the highest potential for determinate value, especially in the initial stages of your journey. The demand consolidation and prioritisation processes outlined in this chapter will help you focus on high-impact initiatives that align with both divisional and corporate strategies.

Finally, the Data Income Statement is a powerful tool to communicate the value generated by your division's data analytics-led initiatives. Tailor this tool to reflect the contributions of your division, allowing you to demonstrate measurable impact to corporate leadership. By addressing these challenges head-on, you can effectively leverage the IFMAPI framework to drive value within your division, ensuring that your efforts are recognised and supported at the corporate level. This approach will not only enhance your division's performance but also strengthen its strategic role within the broader group.

FOUR

Investing In Insights – The 5Rs Framework

Investing in data analytics is the first step in a journey that unlocks transformative value for your company. Success hinges on justifying investments, which requires a blend of data analytics expertise, strategic insight and financial acumen.

When investments in data analytics-led initiatives are driven by hype or isolated IT efforts without clear value realisation, further investment becomes less appealing, eroding data-confidence and leading to risk aversion. Rebuilding this confidence through strategic, value-driven investments can guide your data analytics journey back on track.

This chapter introduces the 5Rs framework – the second key connection for the all-important relationship between the CDAO and CFO. The 5Rs framework requires close involvement from the CFO, enabling confident investments in the data analytics journey by ensuring that investments are justified.

Together, the IFMAPI and 5Rs frameworks provide the foundation to formalise the CDAO–CFO relationship, driving value through data analytics.

Intentions require execution to drive success

To illustrate the importance of execution, we will start this section with a real-life example of a company we have worked with.

CASE STUDY: Missed opportunities

Several years ago, we met with the corporate leadership of a listed group that had been formed through high-value acquisitions. While preparing for the meeting, we noticed a steady decline in their share price over the previous six years since going public. The group had lost 90% of its value over this period!

We were curious about the cause of the decline. They cited external factors like high interest rates, loss of key clients, and the declining economy. However, after some digging, we found the real issue was the lack of execution on a key component of their group strategy: cross-selling services across the group. They admitted that cross-selling – a key strategic driver for forming the group – was not actively pursued or measured.

Two key themes emerge from this example:

1. **Companies must prioritise recognising the value generated from key initiatives.** Using practices like forecasting, measuring and publishing value through a Data Income Statement could have identified the lack of cross-sell success and prompted corrective action, potentially generating millions in shareholder value.

2. **Companies seeking to enhance value by leveraging data must recognise that execution is key.** Steve Jobs, former CEO of Apple Inc., when addressing execution, said that it is a disease to think that a really great idea is 90% of the work key. He said that there is a lot of craftsmanship in between a great idea and a great product.[23]

Innovative ideas are important, but they hold little value without execution. For companies aiming to stay competitive, it is essential to develop a strategy that positions data analytics as a key value driver.

However, without the necessary investment and plan to execute these strategies, even the best ideas will fail to bear fruit.

This chapter will guide you through a framework to prepare your strategy for leveraging data analytics as a key value driver. We will also outline the steps to creating a compelling business case to secure investment for your data analytics journey.

By following our guidance, you should be able to secure the necessary funding to invest in the people, consulting, training and technology essential for launching your value-generating data analytics journey. Applying the concepts from the previous chapter alongside those in this chapter will help you maintain a steady flow of funding as you achieve milestones, enabling you to compound the value you create.

If you already have an established data analytics function, this chapter will help you refine your strategy and enhance your approach to securing ongoing investment. This will enable you to gain further support to extend your value creation and strengthen your competitive edge.

Bridging the investment gap in your data analytics journey

Many years ago, in the early days of IT adoption in companies, business and IT leaders had a more challenging time communicating than they do today. But as time passed, business leaders got exposed to large IT projects like ERP implementations which grew their IT experience, and IT leaders adopted maturing frameworks that helped them explain themselves better. This improved communication between business and IT leaders.

Based on research cited before, we are still in the early days of the adoption of value-driving data analytics in companies. C-level executives lacking knowledge of the data analytics domain hire data analytics leaders who struggle to bridge the value gap, leading to strained relationships. The ensuing communication breakdown leads to significant value loss. Instead of embracing data analytics boldly as a key value driver, executives approach it with caution, stifling investments in high-return initiatives that could enhance the company's competitive edge and provide substantial returns. As a result, data analytics leaders are left battling for funding, which strains relationships even further.

Bridging this gap is within your reach. Working closely with your team to expand your collective knowledge and adopt frameworks, such as the one in this chapter, can turn potential value loss into significant gains. This will enable you to engage with strong data analytics leaders who understand the language and importance of value.

Meanwhile, data analytics leaders need to focus on high-value strategic initiatives and treat stakeholders like investors, using frameworks like the one explained in this and the previous chapter to deliver high-quality pitches and provide regular feedback on value recognised.

The strategic role of the CFO as investment gatekeeper

Among all the C-level executives, the CFO requires the most attention from data analytics leaders. The important KPI for CFOs is financial results. Data analytics leaders must translate their work into this KPI to gain the CFO's support, which is crucial for securing backing for data analytics investments from the CEO and other executives. They all rely on the CFO as a trusted adviser for investment matters.

Even with the CFO as gatekeeper, companies sometimes make investments in data analytics-led initiatives with intuitive approvals based on weak business cases that don't inspire much confidence in the potential for value creation. CFOs need to demand strong,

well-crafted business cases before approving investments rather than approving investments based on
hype or fear of missing opportunities. Do not miss this
red flag. A business case that leaves you with a sense
of discomfort indicates that it is an initiative that will
likely generate only indeterminate value. Instead of
caving in, guide your data analytics leaders towards
improving their approach, as detailed in Chapter
Three, to identify initiatives with a clear pathway to
determinate value.

When CDAOs and data analytics teams fail to support their CFOs in driving value, data analytics
functions are often relegated to merely supporting roles, being caught up in the busy-work of producing insights, rather than being recognised as
core value-creating capabilities. This can lead to an
increased funding risk where the value generated
is questioned. CDAOs need to ensure they generate
determinate value, aligning their initiatives closely
with strategic objectives.

On the other hand, CFOs should follow the principle that applies in law: *ignorantia juris non excu-
sat* – ignorance of law excuses no one. Ignorance
of data analytics concepts is no longer an excuse.
As the gatekeepers of investment, your level of
data-confidence is a critical success factor. The stakes
are high – you might approve a doomed investment
or block one that could be highly lucrative. Becoming
data value-savvy to improve your participation in

the relationships with your data analytics leaders is now more crucial than ever for the sustainability of your company.

The 5Rs framework for investing in insights

With the vital need for high-quality pitching established and the CFO identified as the primary gatekeeper, we can dive into the 5Rs framework for *investing in insights*. This framework will significantly boost your success in pitching for data analytics investments.

The 5 Rs in this framework refer to:

1. Readiness

2. Ringleader

3. Results

4. Roadmap

5. ROI

The diagram below outlines the components of the 5Rs framework.

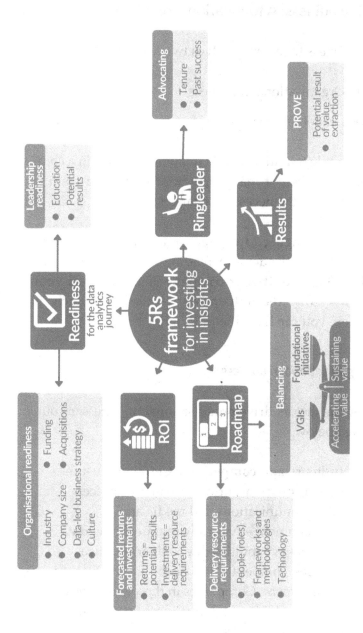

The 5Rs framework for investing in insights

1. Readiness: A foundational requirement

Readiness to invest involves two key aspects:

- Organisational readiness
- Leadership readiness

It is futile to initiate a data analytics journey in a company that is not ready or whose leadership team is resistant to the necessary changes.

It is challenging to change organisational readiness quickly, but leadership readiness can be more easily influenced. If your company is ready, direct your efforts towards influencing leadership, which is where you can have the most impact.

Organisational readiness

Several factors drive organisational readiness, as outlined below.

- **Industry and competitors:** Certain industries – such as pharmaceuticals, financial services, telecommunications and media and entertainment – naturally require strong data analytics capabilities due to their products, services, competitor landscape and regulatory environment. Companies in these industries usually exhibit a high readiness for a formalised data analytics journey.

- **Company size:** Many companies become victims of their success – their increasing complexity hinders further progress, like running into invisible walls, necessitating a formalised data analytics journey to sustain success.

- **Digital-native and data-led businesses:** Companies that rely heavily on data analytics – whether for enhancing existing offerings or selling enriched datasets – are naturally ready for a data analytics journey.

- **Business strategy and high-value use cases:** Companies with a clear strategy and specific data analytics-driven opportunities are well positioned to embark on a data analytics journey.

- **Funding:** Secured funding enables companies to invest in data analytics, enhancing business models and driving new or expanded revenue streams to generate returns for investors.

- **Acquisitions:** Acquisitions introduce three key readiness factors for a data analytics journey:

  1. Gaining visibility into the new acquisition's performance

  2. Providing data analytics services to subsidiaries to achieve strong returns

  3. Consolidating data assets for cross-sell and upsell initiatives as well as other initiatives that benefit from leveraging economies of scale

- **Culture:** Companies with a culture that embraces risk, innovation and data analytics-driven decision-making, especially when supported by adequate funding, are more likely to be ready for a data analytics journey.

ASSESS YOUR VALUE POTENTIAL

Evaluate your company's potential to generate value through a data analytics journey with our Potential for Strategic Value Scorecard. It takes only a few minutes to complete, and you will receive:

- A score per factor
- An overall score
- Further information based on your score

Access the scorecard here:
rappidvaluecycle.com/potentialforvalue

Leadership readiness

Influencing leadership readiness involves two key strategies:

1. **Producing potential results of value extraction (PROVE).** Potential results from data analytics-led initiatives increases leadership's appetite for investment. We will explore how to generate potential results in the upcoming 'Results' section.

2. **Educating leaders about potential value.**
   Highlighting the potential value of a data
   analytics journey is crucial. Showing
   open-minded leaders relevant examples of
   success in similar companies and aligning
   those examples with your company's strategic
   objectives can spark their interest and willingness
   to invest.

With your company and leadership ready, it is time to
move on to identifying a ringleader.

2. Ringleader: The advocate for value-driving insights

A data analytics ringleader is a recognised champion
and advocate for driving value through data analytics. This individual needs influence at the highest
decision-making level as a sponsor and motivator
for investment in the data analytics journey, ensuring
strong support.

Senior leaders who can influence their peers are ideal.
Due to their ability to influence priorities, executives
from finance, strategy or operations are often suitable
candidates to play this role alongside their current
responsibilities.

Tenure can significantly impact a leader's success
as a ringleader, particularly in high-trust cultures. If
a leader is relatively new to the company, a proven

track record in generating value through data analytics becomes crucial to securing trust.

Although the CDAO might seem the obvious choice for ringleader, there are compelling reasons to consider other executives. First, the average CDAO tenure is only two and a half years, compared with five years for other CxOs.[24] Their shorter tenure often weakens CDAOs' influence in the boardroom.

Also, CDAOs with a technical background may struggle to translate complex data analytics concepts in a way that resonates with other executives. This communication gap will hinder their effectiveness as a ringleader, making an alternative executive a better choice for this role.

The ringleader's role is multifaceted, including:

- Identifying high-value data analytics use cases

- Selecting use cases to demonstrate potential results (required in the next section)

- Supporting the preparation and presentation of investment pitches

Choosing a data-confident leader from your executive team for this role is crucial. The most effective ringleaders are data-confident CEOs who set the data analytics vision for their companies. CEOs like Walmart's Doug McMillon, Salesforce's Marc Benioff and Netflix's Reed Hastings, who deeply immersed themselves in their companies' data analytics-driven strategies, exemplify ideal choices for this role. When a CEO not only buys into but also actively drives the company's vision, it paves the way for confident progress in this new direction, as it is backed by strong leadership support.

With a suitable ringleader in place, the next step is to PROVE the value of selected initiatives.

3. Results: PROVE – potential result of value extraction

To gain approval for data analytics investments, it is necessary to demonstrate the potential result of value extraction. Thanks to those initial letters making up the perfect acronym, we say you must PROVE the value. Business leaders weigh up risks when making investment decisions, and they therefore require an evidence-based view of potential outcomes. This approach ensures they feel confident in their decisions. The value proposition must be unmistakable, particularly for leaders who are not data value-savvy.

An investment presentation must rely on more than vague ideas. It requires solid evidence of achievable results that are aligned with the company's strategic goals. For revenue-generating opportunities, evidence might come from:

- Market research

- Competitor analysis

- Customer feedback

- Proof of value (POV) results

For cost-saving initiatives, evidence should include thorough analysis such as:

- Competitor benchmarking

- Root cause analysis

- POV outcomes

Since the CFO is the gatekeeper, securing their approval of the evidence before presenting it to a broader executive audience increases the chances of success.

Selecting high-impact initiatives for evaluation

In Chapter Three's 'Identify value' section we covered the process of demand consolidation to gather your value-generating initiatives, allowing you to select those that are potentially high-impact.

Again, your objective for data analytics-led initiatives must be to generate determinate value and not simply to produce actionable insights. It is therefore important that any potential result clearly demonstrates determinate value. Proposing a dashboard that generates indeterminate value will not cut it.

With guidance from your ringleader and other stakeholders, choose those initiatives with the highest potential value impact from your list of value-generating initiatives.

Creating an evidence-based view to engage stakeholders

We will explain the process of producing the potential result of value extraction by referring back to the 'Top-twenty customer dashboard' example from Chapter Three. We have intentionally used that simplified example again here to make the point that there is value in simple solutions. Innovation is not always valuable, and value does not always have to rely on innovation. Value is less dependent on the complexity of the analytics models and more dependent on how the results are applied in business applications and business processes to drive value-generating actions taken within the window of maximum value, at the coalface of the business.

The 'Top-twenty customer dashboard' example demonstrated how simply identifying your top twenty customers by revenue yields limited value. The real value is unlocked when you compare this data month over month, identify any declines, and investigate the reasons behind those declines. The key takeaway was that insights must be applied. Without corresponding actions – such as offering an alternative product to a declining customer – the value remains indeterminate.

This shift will build stakeholder confidence in the potential results, increasing the likelihood of investment. A forecast based on the above example demonstrates PROVE – the potential result of value extraction.

Generating evidence for potential results with a POV

You may have experience in implementing a data analytics POV. The results were likely disappointing, as they often are. Many POVs fall short because they often demonstrate indeterminate value only, leaving stakeholders uncertain about the potential results.

How do you ensure a POV produces positive results that enable you to move to the next phase, gaining investment approval?

Selecting the right initiative is essential, and your ringleader can provide important guidance. The above example was simplified, but the principles apply equally to enterprises with large customer bases. When executing a POV investigating customer drop-offs in a large enterprise, follow a similar approach:

- Obtain a customer list

- Identify revenue drop-offs month to month

- Find the reasons for the drop-offs

- Propose corrective actions with input from business stakeholders

- Forecast the potential impact of these actions

- Publish the potential results

If greater comfort is required, the results of a sample of corrective actions can provide a better indication of potential success rates.

The approach is similar for executing a different POV that investigates the implementation of a new data analytics-based product to generate a new revenue stream. Rather than focusing on how advanced data analytics or AI techniques could be used to deliver profound insights through the new product, your executive team would place much higher value on your understanding of customer demand and product–market fit for the new product. It is important to know where to focus your efforts when preparing for a new data analytics-driven product presentation, thinking more like an entrepreneur than a data scientist.

After producing the potential results of value extraction for several high-impact value-generating initiatives, the next step is to develop a roadmap for your data analytics journey.

4. Roadmap: Navigating the perilous journey successfully

Just as you need a map for a road trip, a roadmap for a data analytics journey is essential. It needs to include three main components:

1. Value-generating initiatives

2. Foundational initiatives

3. Delivery resource requirements

After defining these, they need to be consolidated and aligned, which we will explore next.

Value-generating initiatives

In Chapter Three we covered the demand consolidation process, which guides the identification and initial prioritisation of value-generating initiatives, which are the foundation of your roadmap. Now we'll consider which value-generating initiatives should be added to the roadmap, and in what order.

Having identified the potential result of value extraction for certain initiatives in the 'Results: PROVE' section above, you now have a detailed view of the potential of each high-impact value-generating initiative. These results can drive the prioritisation of initiatives on the roadmap. Prioritisation must also be driven by dependencies between value-generating initiatives and the order of implementation of foundational initiatives.

Chapter Six will introduce the SCRAPPAD framework to keep this list (or roadmap) updated, ensuring ongoing prioritisation, execution and alignment of initiatives.

Foundational initiatives

Though often overlooked, foundational initiatives are critical for sustaining and growing the value of your data analytics journey. They must be included in your roadmap.

Many companies start their data analytics journey simply, much like planning a straightforward holiday (or vacation). As more elements are added – like multiple families or vehicles – the complexity increases, requiring more preparation and better communication. The families might even need to appoint a 'project manager' to coordinate intricate arrangements.

Similarly, generating value at the start of a data analytics journey is relatively easy. However, scaling and sustaining value over time is an entirely different challenge due to the instability that stems from increasing complexity, with new risks like key-person dependencies and rising data platform costs.

Complexity often arises in data analytics journeys when companies face regulatory or ethics-related data management issues such as data privacy. In a simple environment data privacy is easy enough to manage, and complex processes would be overkill, just as you wouldn't need complicated organisational techniques to plan a simple holiday.

While managing data privacy for a single system may be simple, it becomes exponentially more complex with multiple systems and solutions. Managing data privacy across many systems demands greater planning and integration.

For larger companies, a data analytics journey resembles managing a vast transportation network rather than a simple road trip. The initial part of the journey may seem straightforward, leading to compromises in key processes to keep costs low and delivery speed high. These early compromises are vital for momentum but will lead to a situation where maintenance costs eventually outweigh the value generated. At that point you face a difficult choice: retrofit or shut down. Both are costly and painful.

Since shutting down is not an option, retrofitting is inevitable, but it is expensive and disrupts progress. It's like lifting a house to repair its foundation – a near-impossible feat. This prospect is rarely welcomed by stakeholders, who demand ongoing progress and do not find pleasure in the surprise costs of having to retrofit foundational improvements.

This dilemma often traps data professionals because they are prevented from making essential foundational improvements due to the unexpected costs, and loss of progress, from doing so. To avoid this costly and frustrating scenario, it is vital to focus on foundational initiatives in your roadmap.

Delivery resource requirements

For each value-generating and foundational initiative, you need to identify the required delivery resources:

- People (roles)

- Consulting and training needs for frameworks or methodologies

- Tools (technology) needed for implementation

Conduct a thorough analysis of your existing environment to determine which people, frameworks, methodologies and tools are already available and which are required. Roadmap planning should distinguish between new and existing resources to prioritise initiatives cost-effectively.

As mentioned before, it is a common but tragic mistake to set the objective of a data analytics initiative as the delivery of actionable insights. In this case, you are destined to deliver only indeterminate value. To deliver determinate value, you must set, as your objective, the measurement and publishing of value generated. As highlighted previously, the investments required to generate determinate value are broader than those required to generate indeterminate value, which typically requires only data analytics capabilities. Having already produced the potential result of value extraction, you will be more aware of the effort required to produce determinate value through your high-impact value-generating initiatives. You have gone beyond simply planning to produce actionable insights and built your knowledge of the business processes that will need to change (in collaboration with the relevant business functions) and the integrations into business applications that will be required (in collaboration with your IT department) to generate determinate value.

The integration of insights often requires greater effort than producing insights, and these broader delivery resource requirements must be catered for. Additionally, ensure that you plan for measuring and publishing the value realised. Otherwise, your next investment pitch will be unnecessarily challenging.

After establishing delivery resource requirements, develop specific delivery resource plans:

- A recruitment plan for people

- A consulting and training plan for adopting frameworks and methodologies

- An implementation plan for tools

- An integration plan for embedding analytics results in business processes

These plans should all be integrated with the roadmap.

Roadmap consolidation and alignment

The final step is aligning value-generating initiatives, foundational initiatives and delivery resource plans, which can be a fairly complex undertaking. A successful roadmap effectively balances the delivery of value-generating initiatives with the implementation of foundational initiatives. This ensures that both value realisation and long-term sustainability are prioritised, especially considering that complexity increases along the journey. To achieve the right balance, a senior data strategist experienced in managing rising complexity is essential.

The timing of incorporating foundational initiatives is also crucial. Missing foundational elements early on can lead to costly retrofits later. Engaging an expert who knows how to balance acceleration with confidence can make the difference between success and failure.

'Give me six hours to chop down a tree, and I will spend the first four sharpening the axe.' This saying, in various forms and sources, aptly illustrates the importance of careful planning and timing when implementing foundational initiatives in your data analytics journey.

5. ROI: The bottom-line impact

ROI is the key metric for executives deciding on investments. A comprehensive ROI model typically forecasts returns from value-generating initiatives over three to five years and includes the required investments in people, consulting and technology.

If you have applied the 5Rs framework up to this point, building an ROI model will be straightforward. If you have developed the potential result of value extraction for several of your high-impact value-generating initiatives and applied the methods from Chapter Three for forecasting the potential returns, you will have the returns side of the ROI model already established. For the investment side, to deliver determinate value, you need to convert your detailed plans – developed for delivery resource requirements – into costing calculations (budgets) that include the broader resource requirements beyond just data analytics capabilities.

Combining those components into a financial forecast will produce a solid ROI model.

Stacking returns for investment justification

There is another important reason to build and maintain a comprehensive ROI model for your data analytics journey. The required investments often exceed the forecasted value for a specific initiative. In such cases an approval committee is likely to decline the investment, and rightfully so.

This scenario is common in data analytics journeys, usually because of the need to retrofit foundational elements. It can also occur at the start of the journey, and it has the potential to derail the allocation of investment for potentially high-impact opportunities.

For example, in a subscription-revenue business (like SaaS, telecommunications or media and entertainment), you might aim to protect revenue by building a customer churn analytics model to power targeted retention efforts. This requires consolidating customer data – customer satisfaction, payments, customer service interactions, billing information, product information, etc – across multiple platforms. This can be costly, and the value expected from such an initiative might not justify the investment required. How do you secure funding in such cases? Abandoning the initiative is not ideal, especially if you had anticipated an impactful outcome, as seen with successful churn analytics models at other companies.

To secure the necessary investments, present a holistic view of potential returns from various initiatives that share the same foundational needs. Understanding comprehensive demand is key to obtaining the required investment. If a refresher is required, refer to the demand consolidation exercise in Chapter Three's 'Identify value' section.

Applying the *economies of scale principle* to your data analytics roadmap will justify substantial investments. Identify all value-generating initiatives in your consolidated demand list that rely on the same foundational needs as the customer churn analytics initiative. These could include initiatives like pricing optimisation, cash collection optimisation, and cross-sell initiatives. Stack (or consolidate) the forecasted value from multiple initiatives to build a strong business case for investment. If the returns across all initiatives outweigh the required investments, you are off to the races.

Phasing is key to success and sustained investment

For the churn analytics model mentioned before, regardless of the allocation of funding, phase the development of the consolidated customer view. Start with the most critical component – such as customer satisfaction – and build the churn analytics model around it. Despite your discomfort, bring the initial solution into production to prove its value early and gather insights for improvement. Once the value is demonstrated, iterate to the next phase of consolidation and enhancement. This phased approach manages risk, satisfies stakeholders and eases investment decisions.

Now that we have been through the 5Rs, we will look at how to prepare for an investment pitch by combining the 5Rs and IFMAPI frameworks.

Integrating the 5Rs and IFMAPI frameworks for sustained success

The 5Rs and IFMAPI frameworks are complementary tools that align investing and value realisation in data analytics journeys. The 5Rs framework guides companies through the investment stage, ensuring that data analytics-led initiatives are strategically aligned and capable of delivering measurable returns. The IFMAPI framework focuses on continuously measuring, forecasting and communicating the value generated by these initiatives.

By integrating these frameworks, companies can secure and sustain investments in data analytics, creating a continuous cycle of value creation and reinforcement that positions data analytics as a strategic driver of business success.

Preparing to invest in your data analytics journey: A step-by-step guide

The following diagram and the accompanying table integrate the frameworks and principles from this and the previous chapter, offering a step-by-step guide designed to maximise your chances of securing funding.

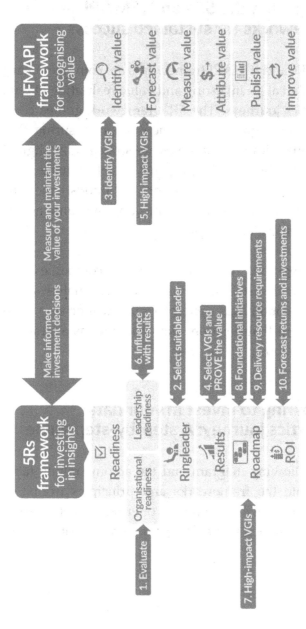

IFMAPI framework for recognising value

- Identify value
- Forecast value
- Measure value
- Attribute value
- Publish value
- Improve value

3. Identify VGIs

5. High impact VGIs

Measure and maintain the value of your investments

Make informed investment decisions

5Rs framework for investing in insights

- ☑ Readiness
  - Organisational readiness
  - Leadership readiness
- Ringleader
- Results
- Roadmap
- ROI

6. Influence with results

2. Select suitable leader

4. Select VGIs and PROVE the value

8. Foundational initiatives

9. Delivery resource requirements

10. Forecast returns and investments

1. Evaluate

7. High-impact VGIs

The ten steps to obtain funding for your data analytics journey

Step no.	Description	Related framework component
1	Evaluate organisational readiness and leadership readiness.	5Rs framework: Readiness
2	Select a suitable ringleader who will provide input into the strategy and high-impact initiatives.	5Rs framework: Ringleader
3	Work with stakeholders to identify value-generating initiatives.	IFMAPI framework: Identify value
4	Select high-impact value-generating initiatives with guidance from the ringleader, then PROVE the value (generate potential results of value extraction).	5Rs framework: Results
5	Forecast the value from the results of high-impact value-generating initiatives. If executing a POV to generate evidence of potential results: measure, attribute and publish the value of the POV.	IFMAPI framework: Forecast value Measure value Attribute value Publish value
6	Use the forecasted value of the high-impact value-generating initiatives and combine with leadership education to influence leadership readiness.	5Rs framework: Readiness
7	Add the relevant high-impact value-generating initiatives to the roadmap.	5Rs framework: Roadmap

Step no.	Description	Related framework component
8	Determine the foundational initiatives for the roadmap and align these with the value-generating initiatives. Remember to include a foundational initiative for establishing the IFMAPI framework to measure, publish and improve the value of initiatives.	5Rs framework: Roadmap
9	Determine the delivery resource requirements for the roadmap (for value-generating initiatives and foundational initiatives).	5Rs framework: Roadmap
10	Using the principles from forecast value, build the returns forecast for the ROI model. Then forecast the investments required for delivery resource requirements (people, consulting and technology) to add to the ROI model.	5Rs framework: ROI

While the ten steps primarily address companies without a data analytics function, they can easily be adapted for companies with existing functions that struggle to demonstrate value and consistently face challenges in justifying investments. If this applies to you, reflect on how your company could have better implemented these concepts as you work through the ten steps. Make necessary adjustments and reevaluate your investment strategy to accelerate your data analytics journey more confidently.

Key considerations for securing investment in your data analytics journey

Stakeholders should be treated like investors who are focused on safeguarding both the company's and their own reputations. Approach the pitch for investment in a data analytics journey as if you were pitching to external investors considering a new venture. How does this perspective influence your approach?

The business case for investing in data analytics must be clearly articulated, with compelling justification that aligns with the company's strategic objectives and clearly demonstrates the potential value.

While this approach works well for CxOs with experience in startups and scaleups, it may not resonate as strongly with those who have only ever operated in corporate environments. In corporate settings, shareholder management often appears more straightforward than investment management. This crucial distinction highlights the difference between a CxO acting as a custodian of business assets on behalf of shareholders, versus the CxO with an investment mindset involving ventures that require a greater risk appetite than may be tolerated by the average corporate CxO.

Starting with nothing is inherently riskier than starting with something – a reality often misunderstood in corporate spheres. The data analytics journey is more like the former – starting with nothing – and must therefore be treated accordingly, with the investment pitch being prepared more as if you were presenting to a venture capitalist than an institutional investor.

The CFO, thinking more like a venture capitalist, must thoroughly evaluate the business case and integrate it into the financial plan. As the gatekeeper of financial discipline, the CFO's endorsement is crucial. Their support, combined with that of an influential ring-leader who advocates for the initiative, will be essential to securing broader executive approval.

If the pitch provides clear evidence of potential value and appropriate risk mitigation and is delivered convincingly, the only thing holding you back from an approval will be the data-confidence of your leadership team.

Common pitfalls and how to avoid them

Many business leaders are not data value-savvy, just as many data leaders are not business-savvy. A common pitfall is that investment pitches focus too much on the *how* rather than on the value. When the discussion shifts to how problems will be solved or how solutions will be built, the focus on the value of solving these problems is lost. It is crucial to refocus on the value to be generated and how risks will be mitigated.

Questions about how problems will be solved or how solutions will be built are normal. Provide supporting information to answer these questions while keeping in mind that, without relevant domain experience, some details may be unfamiliar to the audience. Establish confidence that the promised results can be achieved.

Finally, avoid being swayed by technology hype or feeling pressured to make decisions that do not fully align with your comfort level. The business case needs to be robust enough to build confidence in your investment decision. If you are uncomfortable, push back and request the information needed to achieve that level of confidence.

Final thoughts: Strategically investing in your data analytics journey

As we conclude this chapter, envision your data analytics journey as an important and exciting expedition – one where your careful planning and committed execution will lead to rewarding success and a lasting impact on your company. Your success will be determined by the accuracy of your maps, the supplies you pack and the team you assemble. The 5Rs framework is not just a set of guidelines – it is your compass to navigate the complex terrain of investment in data analytics.

The key themes we have explored in this chapter underscore the importance of alignment. Just as a ship's captain will not set sail without a well-planned route, you should not embark on a data analytics journey without a solid strategy that connects intentions with investments. A solid roadmap maintains the right balance between showing quick value and building foundations to sustain and scale the value.

Bridging the gap between data analytics leaders and the CFO ensures that both the navigator and the captain understand the significance of the voyage. Both roles must be aligned – data analytics leaders need to present strong, evidence-based cases, while the CFO must elevate their understanding to enable informed decisions that will steer the company towards value creation.

As you venture forward on this journey, remember that your leadership's readiness is like your vessel's condition – without it, your journey will falter, no matter how promising it had seemed. Selecting the right ringleader as your first mate will help guide the crew through the storms, ensuring that everyone stays the course.

In the next chapter we delve into the foundation of your journey: people. Just as a well-trained crew is essential to a successful voyage, the right team will be crucial in turning your data analytics strategy into a reality. Buckle up – the most exciting part of the journey is still to come.

Key chapter takeaways

- To succeed with data analytics-led initiatives, your ideas, intentions and strategy must align with your investments and execution. This requires evidence-based business cases that deliver company objectives and demonstrate determinate value.

- The 5Rs framework – readiness, ringleader, results, roadmap and ROI – provides a structured approach to secure and sustain investment in data analytics-led initiatives, ensuring they deliver on their promises.

- The 5Rs and IFMAPI frameworks operate hand in hand to strengthen the relationship between the CDAO and CFO, ensuring investments in data analytics are justified and deliver measurable returns.

- Selecting a strong ringleader with influence and data-confidence – preferably a senior leader outside the CDAO role – is essential to advocating for and guiding the data analytics journey.

- Organisational and leadership readiness are foundational for embarking on a data analytics journey. Without them, even the best strategies will falter.

- Producing potential results of value extraction (PROVE) is necessary to build confidence and secure investment, emphasising the importance of selecting high-impact value-generating initiatives.

- A well-balanced roadmap that includes value-generating and foundational initiatives is crucial for ensuring long-term success and avoiding costly retrofits later in the journey. Plans for delivery resource requirements must be integrated.

- ROI models should consolidate the potential returns from multiple initiatives to justify investments, particularly when foundational elements require substantial upfront costs.

A NOTE FOR DIVISIONAL AND SUBSIDIARY LEADERS

The 5Rs framework provides essential strategies for securing and justifying investments in data analytics. As a divisional or subsidiary leader, you may face unique challenges such as limited influence over corporate-level investment decisions, and navigating your division's readiness compared with the broader group.

To overcome these hurdles, it is crucial to align your initiatives with corporate objectives and leverage the support of a ringleader at the corporate level. This ringleader can advocate for your initiatives and help secure the necessary experts, or shared resources, that are suitably qualified and experienced to meet your divisional needs.

Additionally, balancing the need for foundational initiatives with the delivery of quick wins will be vital in sustaining long-term success, while proving the value of your projects in an internal environment competing for funding from one investment pool.

By strategically aligning your efforts with the broader company goals, you can effectively contribute to the success of your division and the group.

FIVE

People And Data Value Culture – The STACKER+DVC Framework

I n today's world everything is driven by data. Information is power. All the data in the world is useless, though, without the key to unlocking its true value: talented data experts.

Data is abundant, much like water on Earth. However, just as most water is not immediately usable or potable, vast amounts of data are of little value before it is processed and refined. Like someone stranded on a remote island, surrounded by ocean water yet dying of thirst because the water is not drinkable, companies can drown in data without seeing any value from it. They lack the expertise to transform it into something valuable.

Talent management

Data analytics professionals are not merely operational staff. They are key to transforming your vast
raw data resources into refined insights that will propel your business forward. There is a global shortage
of these in-demand, highly skilled people. Companies
with strong talent management strategies, especially
strategies for attracting and retaining these experts,
will gain a competitive edge.

However, the concept *Miss by an inch and you'll be off by
a mile* is highly relevant to data analytics talent. Even
small errors early in your journey can have unfore-
seen consequences further down the line. While the
task ahead may seem daunting, by taking one step
at a time and applying the strategies in this chapter,
you can position your team as leaders in achieving
success through data analytics.

People and culture: A unified
ecosystem for data analytics success

To truly unlock the potential of your data analytics
function, you need to bear in mind that people and
culture are deeply interconnected. They function as
one ecosystem. When leaders bring about changes that
positively influence culture, people feel the impact
and reinforce the culture. Recognising this interplay

is essential for driving sustained success in your data analytics-led initiatives.

Suppose that a major leadership change, like the appointment of a new COO, brings a new emphasis on collaboration, transparency and a data analytics-driven approach to decision-making. This leadership style will naturally influence the company's culture, resulting in more open communication, data analytics-driven decisions and better alignment of the team's values with the company's strategic goals. The cultural shift starts to permeate the broader company, enhancing its culture. As a result, people feel more valued and motivated, leading to higher retention rates and stronger overall performance. The people, in turn, reinforce the newly established values, leading to further positive outcomes for the company.

This chapter introduces a framework to drive the setup and effective management of capable data analytics talent operating in a value-driving culture, enabling you to unlock the potential to turn data into a strategic asset that drives long-term success. As a data-confident leader, your role is to unleash this potential by shaping the ecosystem. By consciously driving positive cultural shifts, you can create an environment where your team thrives and your data analytics-led initiatives flourish.

CASE STUDY: A masterclass in managing in-demand talent for sustained success

Many consider Sir Alex Ferguson to be the most successful football/soccer manager of all time and one of the greatest managers in the history of all sports. During his illustrious twenty-seven-year tenure as manager of Manchester United, his team won a record thirteen Premier League titles, two UEFA Champions League titles, five FA Cup titles, and numerous other domestic and international trophies. Who could ever forget the last-minute win over Bayern Munich in the UEFA Champions League Final in 1999? This win saw Manchester United take an unprecedented treble, winning the Premier League, FA Cup and UEFA Champions League all in the same season. What an incredible achievement.

During his tenure, Ferguson managed approximately 1,500 matches. His approach produced consistent results over an extended period.

Ferguson had a unique leadership style. With a keen eye for talent, he formed close personal bonds with star players early in their careers, nurturing them to success. He was instrumental in developing football legends like David Beckham, Ryan Giggs and Cristiano Ronaldo. The United manager fostered team unity and camaraderie that extended beyond the pitch and into players' personal lives. His mentorship established a winning culture, leading many superstar players to stay loyal to Manchester United despite attractive offers from other top clubs.

Ferguson's no-nonsense approach, competitive pay, and career advancement opportunities kept his players motivated, leading to consistent success over many years.

He was a master of structure on and off the field. He experimented with new formations to outwit opponents, clearly communicated each player's role and strategically positioned his players to maximise their strengths.

In 2003 Ferguson released star player David Beckham, following a serious misdemeanour, prioritising team culture over individual talent. This decision exemplifies Ferguson's approach to key-person dependencies and his belief in the collective strength of the team. His foresight ensured continued success despite Beckham's departure.[25]

With Ferguson having been top manager of some of the highest paid, most in-demand superstars, leading them to sustained success over nearly three decades, his career stands out as a truly remarkable achievement.

With the rising demand for and limited supply of skilled data analytics experts, prioritising their management is crucial to maximising the value your data can generate.

In this chapter we present a framework for building and sustaining a world-class data analytics function and a strong data value culture. You will learn how to:

- Attract top talent

- Foster continuous learning

- Create an environment that maximises efficiency and minimises employee turnover

By prioritising data talent, you unlock a goldmine of value, transforming your data into a strategic weapon for long-term success.

The STACKER+DVC framework for people and data value culture

To maximise the value of your data, you first need to maximise the potential of your people. The STACKER+DVC framework for people and data value culture, shown in the following diagram, includes key components essential for optimising your data superstars.

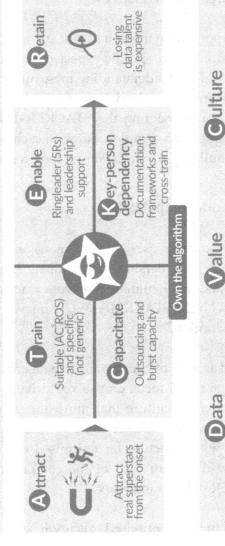

Structure
Strategic weapons not operational resources

Attract
Attract real superstars from the onset

Train
Suitable (AC^{3}ROS) and specific (not generic)

Capacitate
Outsourcing and burst capacity

Own the algorithm

Enable
Ringleader (5Rs) and leadership support

Key-person dependency
Documentation, frameworks and cross-train

Retain
Losing data talent is expensive

Data

Value

Culture

The STACKER+DVC framework for people and data value culture

The STACKER+DVC framework ensures your data talent and culture are optimised to deliver high-value data analytics-led initiatives.

The components of the framework are interconnected, each addressing a specific aspect of managing data analytics talent. Understanding these nuances is vital, as small errors can lead to costly long-term consequences. Implementing the STACKER+DVC framework might seem complex, but with each component you are building a foundation for long-term success.

Framework compatibility

If your company uses a talent management framework like Josh Bersin's New Talent Management Framework, your human resources team can easily align it with the STACKER+DVC framework for simplified adoption.[26]

While all aspects of talent management are important, this chapter will focus on the key drivers of people and data value culture that most impact your ability to realise and sustain value from data analytics. Starting with structure for optimised execution, we will now dive into each of the components of the STACKER+DVC framework:

1. Structure for optimised execution

2. Train for success

3. Attract the right talent

4. Capacitate your teams

5. Key-person dependency risk reduction

6. Enable and support your teams

7. Retain critical skills

8. Data value culture

1. Structure for optimised execution

Imagine an orchestra where each musician plays their own choice of music. The resulting noise would be anything but harmonious – a deafening cacophony. Similarly, a data analytics function without proper structure lacks coordination and focus, making it impossible for value to be unlocked. Optimising the structure of your data analytics function is not a luxury. It is a necessity for generating value.

Identifying structural challenges

If you are experiencing any of the following challenges, it may indicate structural issues in your data analytics function:

- Ineffective delivery
- Data not always easily accessible

- Unclear responsibilities for data analytics and insights

- Executive hesitation to rely on data analytics due to inadequate delivery (e.g., long lead times)

- Uncertainty about team members' capabilities

- Constant pressure on your team to deliver, with ongoing complaints about resource constraints, despite team expansion

- High staff turnover, with people leaving before twenty-four months' tenure

- Difficulty filling vacancies for data professionals

The essential role of structure in driving value

As more people capture, use and distribute data, the risk of failure increases. While managing complex processes and technology is challenging, managing people adds a whole new layer of complexity. Proper structure enables your team to adapt to change and manage this complexity. Restructuring teams may be necessary, but this requires careful planning to avoid costly mistakes.

It takes time for data analytics functions to build momentum. If your data analytics team is not perceived as a strategic value driver, it risks being seen as merely operational, making it vulnerable to frequent restructuring, with little regard to the impact on value creation.

Be mindful of whether your data analytics function is perceived as an operational function or as a strategic value driver. Restructuring disrupts momentum and often leads to increased staff turnover, which is costly, especially given the difficulty of replacing these skilled experts. Carefully consider alternatives before making changes that could have expensive long-term consequences.

A well-embedded structure supports the other STACKER+DVC framework components, including talent attraction and retention. Data analytics experts gravitate towards companies where they feel valued and see direct investment from leadership, and all that begins with a robust structure.

Key structural considerations for data analytics success

Identify which of the following structures best suits your company:

- Centralised
- Decentralised
- Hybrid
- Flat
- Hierarchical
- Self-organising

Your structure needs to align with the team's mandate and with the company's communication framework, business objectives and strategy, ensuring effective allocation of accountability and responsibility.

In teams with high-demand specialists, you might have too many leaders and insufficient hands-on workers. Like Sir Alex Ferguson's Manchester United team, even the most talented individuals must understand their roles within the structure to achieve success. Ensure roles are clear and, if needed, establish temporary accountability or project-specific communication channels, using dotted reporting lines.

Optimise your data analytics structure for efficient resource allocation. This involves distributing multifunctional projects and tasks to the right team members, ensuring capacity is available when needed so that one part of the team does not delay the progress of another. Implementing the SCRAPPAD, DRIVER and DATABRIDGE frameworks (covered in Chapter Six) alongside a well-structured team will enhance delivery speed and output quality, thereby accelerating value realisation.

Consider your company's unique culture when selecting the optimal structure for your data analytics function. What works in a large financial institution with multiple hierarchical levels and specific compliance needs may not suit your company. Instead of directly replicating other companies' structures, adapt them to fit your culture and objectives.

With a formal approach to structuring your data analytics function, you can transform your team from a scattered ensemble into a finely tuned orchestra capable of generating a symphony of data analytics-driven insights. Even minor adjustments to your structure can improve team efficiency and morale. Every step you take towards refining your structure is a step towards unlocking greater value from your data. Structure is the cornerstone of your company's success with data analytics.

2. Train for success

The world evolves constantly. Just as a brain surgeon learning from a 1950s textbook would struggle with modern neurology, clinging to outdated skills in data analytics is risky. Without active training in relevant business and data competencies, your ability to realise value from data analytics will be severely limited.

Why training is fundamental for success

Research shows that companies that train employees in data analytics skills consistently outperform those that do not.[27] This makes sense because a financial manager with data analytics skills is a better financial manager, a marketer with data analytics skills is a better marketer, and so on. When more employees understand data, more opportunities will be found for data analytics-driven value creation. However, the real challenge is teaching those employees to focus on value creation, which requires specific training.

Data analytics functions often focus on data without considering its impact on business priorities and value. Your data analytics function must become business-savvy and understand key value drivers to create real value. While the data analytics function may push for everyone to be trained on data, they also need training on business objectives and concepts. This requires continuous attention.

Key training considerations

Embedding learning into your company's approach creates more opportunities for value creation. If your data skills training is haphazard, work with your talent management team to improve this.

Data skills training often targets only technical staff, which remains important for adopting the latest technologies and methodologies. However, training should also include a broader range of employees, helping them understand how their roles can contribute to data analytics-driven value creation.

Avoid shortcuts without a clear strategy, such as generic online courses, which waste resources that could be better spent elsewhere. Training needs to be tailored to your company's specific needs, based on a well-crafted learning and development strategy that aligns with strategic objectives and focuses on the required skills. Remember: Sir Alex Ferguson's success resulted from him meticulously planning training to develop his players into superstars.

For data analytics-led initiatives to succeed, training must be integrated into your delivery processes. As workflows and decision-making processes change to drive value from data analytics-led initiatives, those affected in planning and implementation must be involved, securing their buy-in and ownership.

Without proper communication and training, resistance to process changes can lead to the failure of potentially lucrative initiatives. Effective change management must include training for a broad range of people, including:

- Those building or configuring solutions
- Users of the solutions
- Stakeholders from other areas affected by the changes

Key training interventions

Consider three main training interventions:

1. Assessing your skills inventory and gaps
2. Developing a comprehensive learning strategy focused on agility and aligned to your company's strategic goals

3. Promoting a learning culture in your data analytics function and senior leadership to align everyone with leveraging data for value creation and acceleration

Like a robust structure, training is a powerful tool for attracting and retaining talent. Prioritising intentional learning transforms your data analytics function from stagnation into a dynamic, evolving force, ready to unlock your data's true potential. This fuels your company's data value-driven journey, propelling you towards transformative results.

3. Attract the right talent

Attracting talented data experts is one of the most challenging yet essential aspects of a successful data analytics journey. These highly skilled professionals can unlock a treasure trove of insights that:

- Fuel innovation

- Optimise operations

- Drive strategic decisions

- Increase revenue

- Reduce risk

Data professionals want to be challenged by their work and they want to feel valued. To attract top talent, position your company as an industry leader that genuinely relies on employees' skills to deliver on its innovative vision and roadmap.

Identifying valuable data experts

Like a sports manager identifying key talent, your success depends on recognising and attracting the right data experts.

In our view, the most important characteristic of a data expert is how drawn they are towards translating routine tasks into standardised, repeatable processes that can be automated. They have a framework-driven mindset. This capability is especially valuable because it accelerates delivery. It also reduces technology costs. A framework-driven mindset means that tools are purchased to automate and accelerate processes rather than for fancy new features that will likely never be used.

Standardising processes brings consistency, which accelerates time-to-value and reduces implementation and maintenance costs. These superstars transform complex tasks into easily repeatable activities, enhancing business continuity and reducing key-person dependencies by creating clear, repeatable structures for the team.

Attracting the right talent positions your company as an innovation powerhouse. If you are unsure how to identify the necessary skills for your data analytics roadmap, consider partnering with an experienced data expert. This is a critical decision, with long-term consequences for mistakes.

Sourcing data analytics talent: strategies and challenges

You have three options for acquiring talent:

1. Growing skills organically through bursaries and internships, and developing existing staff

2. Hiring existing skills from the market

3. Outsourcing specific roles, with a formal strategy to manage this effectively

Optimise your hiring processes to enable you to act quickly. Data experts are in high demand and often engage with multiple companies when job hunting. If you can't close a critical hire in less than a month, you risk losing candidates to competitors with faster processes.

When hiring data experts, remember that your competition is not limited to your industry or region. Cross-industry appointments and remote work are common, making it harder to secure top talent.

While there are other interventions to consider, these are in our experience the most effective. While finding the right talent can be challenging, applying the STACKER+DVC framework will increase your chances of finding the right people who share your vision and drive.

4. Capacitate your teams

Your ability to generate value through data analytics-led initiatives will depend on the capacity of your data analytics function. As a business leader, you must champion the importance of adequately capacitating these critical teams, based on a strategic approach.

The importance of capacitating your teams

When business priorities change, the prioritisation and expectation management processes of a data analytics function can take strain under the pressure of demanding stakeholders. Data experts are frequently caught in the trap of diverted focus and multiple conflicting priorities, leading to overwork that can cause burnout and increased staff turnover.

Sir Alex Ferguson used squad rotation to ensure his star players rested. In the long term, this proved to be the better choice rather than squeezing the life out of his players to achieve short-term success. His broader team of 'workhorse players' was always ready to step in. As a result, the team were able to sustain success.

Your data analytics function needs options to increase capacity, whether permanently or temporarily, through contracting or outsourcing. Ideally, they should have an accelerated route to secure funding to meet business demands without constant pressure.

You must consider and remove the roadblocks to introducing additional capacity by focusing on the value that these investments will generate. Remember, when value forecasting is trusted, approvals for capacity investments will be straightforward.

To build your in-house capabilities, focus on accelerating your hiring processes. Align early with senior leadership (CEO, CFO and CHRO) on capacity requirements. Delays in capacitating your teams might see you losing employees faster than you can hire new people.

Owning the algorithm: A strategic approach to delivering data analytics

Some companies use a blended approach, outsourcing for experimentation and short-term projects, and making permanent appointments once the function matures and generates sustainable value. This allows you to focus on niche components of value creation while outsourcing areas that do not require deep business context, such as platform management, application support and some data engineering capabilities. This way, your teams can concentrate on what brings the most value.

In digital transformation this approach is known as *owning the algorithm*. Focus on capabilities that allow you to own the algorithm. Commoditised needs can be procured more cost-effectively. Owning the algorithm provides the most value, and this needs to be your primary focus.

By proactively addressing your team's capacity needs, you are setting up for success. Your foresight and action in this area will ensure that your data analytics function is not merely reactive. It will be leading the charge in growing your company.

5. Key-person dependency risk reduction

Data is central to your company's success, but key-person dependency within your data analytics function is a hidden vulnerability. It occurs when progress relies on the knowledge and expertise of specific individuals. While those people are valuable, depending solely on them poses a risk – if they leave, critical projects could stall and value creation could suffer. Fortunately, you can proactively mitigate this risk.

David Beckham's unexpected departure from Manchester United in 2003 occurred because Sir Alex Ferguson prioritised team culture over individual star power. Ferguson understood that the team's success was more important than any one player, and he had already prepared to handle such eventualities.[28]

Identifying key-person dependency risks

If you've ever been told *Person X is on leave and will send the data when they return,* you likely have a key-person dependency risk. In our experience, key-person dependencies are common among data analytics function leaders and technical staff.

You risk creating key-person dependencies if you own the entire data analytics value chain, from platform support to data engineers, data modellers and analysts, because you will have limited redundancy between team members that are spread thin across many different systems, business functions and areas of responsibility. However, if you focus on functions that directly own the algorithm and outsource the rest, you pass on the redundancy issue, reduce risk and make managing key-person dependencies easier.

You face key-person dependency risks in your data science and business intelligence roles, and in other data functions, but this risk usually affects the data engineering team the most. Typically, one individual or a small group in this team holds most of the institutional knowledge. They are often overworked and underpaid, and they feel undervalued. Senior leaders are usually aware, as they are regularly reminded that they cannot afford to lose these key individuals.

When these key individuals become unhappy at work, they start exploring other opportunities. Retention becomes nearly impossible as they demand a higher salary than you can afford to offer. You might have to contract them at a much higher rate to retain their knowledge or counter their offers. However, counter-offering is like sticking a Band-Aid on a fracture – 80% of employees who accept a counter-offer leave within a year.[29]

Long-term commitment is unlikely once the relationship is broken, making departure almost inevitable. Simply paying someone more will not alleviate job pressure, and the risk of losing their knowledge remains. Addressing the root cause is essential to prevent these issues from hindering progress.

Proactively mitigating key-person dependency risks

Key-person dependency is a common issue in data analytics, often due to poor talent management and a lack of standards. It creates significant costs and risks for the company, so proactive management is essential.

Strategies to mitigate key-person dependency risk include:

1. Cross-train team members to perform critical tasks.

2. Document all work, follow formal frameworks and apply standardised methodologies

(see Chapter Six). This also facilitates easier onboarding of new people.

3. Develop a succession plan, and ensure capacity is available for key roles if critical team members exit.

4. Consider outsourcing to reduce reliance on highly skilled, high-cost individuals prone to turnover.

5. Ensure outsourcing agreements include knowledge management requirements such as documenting key processes and institutional knowledge.

6. If losing a single team member would harm delivery, consider creating spare capacity, especially in critical roles.

7. Obtain key-person insurance to manage the financial risk of replacing a critical team member at a higher cost.

In our experience, critical staff – especially engineers – can unlock substantial value. By implementing cross-training and thorough documentation, you can transform a potential vulnerability into a strength, ensuring your team's resilience and continuity.

6. Enable and support your teams

Data analytics functions cannot achieve strategic objectives alone. When operating in isolation, they typically provide data extracts, reports and some insights. To succeed with generating determinate value, they require support from cross-functional teams.

Challenges faced by data analytics functions without support

When priorities shift, cost-cutting often begins with data-related projects, followed by IT and then business projects. This sequence is driven by a lack of confidence in value realisation. Business functions usually articulate expected value clearly. IT functions can do this to some extent, but data analytics functions often struggle with value forecasting and stakeholders with low levels of data-confidence. A lot of their work generates indeterminate value, and they rely on the success of IT and business projects to realise determinate value. We address solutions to this challenge in Chapters Three and Nine.

Data analytics projects are, therefore, usually targets to be deprioritised first. Data analytics functions that can better articulate their value proposition will likely gain more stakeholder support. However, given the reliance that data analytics functions have on IT and business functions to realise value, business leaders must consider the support required for data analytics to demonstrate value. Slowing down investment could have substantial long-term impacts, so cutting is not always the best decision.

As a business leader, you should ensure the following key support features are in place for the success of your data analytics functions:

- Lead by example. Show your team that you value data analytics and rely on it for value creation, which will encourage others to collaborate with the data analytics function.

- Ensure your data analytics function has a clear mandate from senior management, aligning their role with company expectations.

- Provide executive sponsorship. As discussed in Chapter Four, the ringleader role is crucial in supporting the data analytics function.

- Avoid micromanagement by establishing formal success measures and clear accountability.

- Promote knowledge sharing and showcase the value the data analytics function brings.

- Publicly acknowledge the data analytics function's contributions to the company's value creation.

Open and effective communication between data analytics leaders, senior stakeholders and other decision-makers is essential for consistent alignment of objectives. Data analytics leaders need a clear mandate aligned with their role, and like any team, they require adequate support from company leadership to succeed.

Companies hedge important initiatives by investing through multiple streams, creating redundancy because leadership is unwilling to assign the primary mandate to their data analytics function. With multiple horses in the race, this creates the perception that no specific horse receives full support, hindering the success of the data analytics function.

Teams in the business must collaborate, with leaders leveraging their strengths and empowering them to succeed rather than pitting them against each other. Competing efforts will lead to shadow data analytics teams that appear when data analysts are appointed by managers in business functions that are not sanctioned for this type of role. This leads to silos that increase cost and limit value creation.

To avoid this, as a business leader you need to make time available for feedback, reducing pressure from demanding stakeholders on the data analytics function, and allowing roadblocks to be escalated and resolved quickly. Communicate your expectation for regular feedback on project progress through formal channels, and maintain these disciplines even during lengthy projects.

Your support can be the catalyst for your team's success. You empower your team to reach their full potential by actively engaging with them and removing obstacles, driving your data analytics-led initiatives to new heights.

7. Retain critical skills

Losing critical skills impacts not only remuneration costs but also your ability to realise value, which can be even more costly. Retention must therefore be a priority.

Retention is easier in a winning team. With Sir Alex Ferguson as manager, Manchester United could offer superstar footballers high salaries and the satisfaction of being part of a winning team. If your data analytics function is not adding substantial value, a losing culture sets in, meaning that offering higher salaries will not be enough to retain key staff members. Retention becomes an unsolvable challenge. If this is your situation, address the root cause by adjusting your data analytics strategy to focus on generating value.

Retaining critical team members is crucial for the success of your data analytics function. Focusing on a retention strategy is essential if your team generates value, has the right mix of skills and has team members you want to retain.

Remuneration is the most obvious lever for retention. Paying market-related salaries is essential for retaining critical staff, although it is not the only factor.

Business leaders are often surprised by the cost of data experts, typically comparing them to IT experts of similar seniority such as software engineers.

However, data experts are more expensive due to the specialised nature of their work and the skills shortage in this field.

Beyond fair remuneration, focus your retention strategy on giving team members more reasons to stay. Strategies for retaining critical data analytics talent include the following:

- Provide clear purpose, direction and support to help staff deliver value (see 'Enable and support your teams' above).

- Offer access to learning and development opportunities to help staff grow (see 'Train for success' above).

- Establish clear promotion and career development roadmaps.

- Where appropriate, offer performance-based rewards for key team members.

- Implement an operating model that allows for work-life balance. Flexibility can help data experts deliver more effectively. Allow them a level of autonomy in how they work.

- Engage employees through transparent communication from senior leadership, which goes a long way to building trust.

- Implement structures for regular feedback and review, to maintain open communication and quickly resolve challenges.

Retaining your top talent is not just about keeping people – it is about maintaining momentum and ensuring continued innovation. Your efforts in this area will pay dividends as your team grows stronger and more cohesive, driving ongoing success.

8. Data value culture

Culture is a shared set of values, beliefs and behaviours that can be influenced positively or negatively. Data value culture specifically emphasises values, beliefs and behaviours that prioritise the use of data analytics to drive value.

EXAMPLE: A practical illustration of data value culture

Consider an outbound call centre agent whose performance is measured only by sales. With this as their sole success metric, they prioritise selling over accurate data capture. This behaviour negatively impacts the company, leading to poor-quality data that results in operational inefficiencies and downstream failures in potentially high-value data analytics-led initiatives.

If you update the call centre agent's performance plan to include data quality metrics, their sales might initially decline. However, they will eventually adjust and develop new behaviours, and both the agent and the company will benefit from better-quality data.

This scenario helps illustrate why so many data analytics projects fail globally. Companies need to implement basic data quality processes, but many do not because the impacts are only felt much later. Data issues need to be fixed at the source, requiring leadership alignment and consistent application across the company. This is essentially treating your data as an asset.

Contrasting ineffective and effective data value cultures

A weak data value culture is easy to identify, as the symptoms are clear. The following table lists key differences between a poor data value culture and a strong one.

Ineffective data value culture	Effective data value culture
Data is siloed. Data is scattered across departments in unusable formats, making it a burden to manage rather than a value-generating asset.	**Data collaboration is enabled.** Cross-functional data is accessible, usable, and managed as a value-generating asset.
Data is inaccessible. Accessing data is tedious and time-consuming.	**Data is accessible.** Accessing data is quick and easy, with a clear process to follow.
Data trust is low. It is distrusted by default.	**Data is trusted.** It is used to drive value.
Transparency is deficient. Data processing and sharing are limited, with no openness about what has been done with the data or where it came from.	**Transparency exists.** Data origins and processing are openly shared with stakeholders.

Decision-making is impaired. There is a lack of data analytics-driven decision-making, with decisions based mostly on gut feel.	Decision-making is strong. Decision-making is driven by data analytics, reducing reliance on gut feel.

Culture has a broad impact, and misaligned values can have catastrophic results. However, focusing on core factors can drive behaviour changes that lead to data value enablement.

Sir Alex Ferguson used culture as a tool for success. He instilled pride in playing for Manchester United, reminding players of the club's prestigious history, the expectations of wearing the club's jersey, and that they should always give their best, never giving up until the final whistle. This fostered unity and belonging, contributing to the team's success.[30]

Examples of how to stimulate and establish a strong data value culture include:

- Encouraging a data value culture of innovation by allowing teams to experiment and by celebrating failures as learning opportunities.

- Driving a culture of data analytics-driven decision-making by enforcing that all recommendations and decisions are based on reliable data. Leaders must discipline themselves to question assumptions and consider alternatives before acting.

- Encouraging a data value culture focused on realising value by enabling teams to develop strong business cases for data analytics-led initiatives, building confidence in investment decisions.

- Encouraging a culture of openness and transparency, where data is trusted, by adopting formal data management frameworks and processes aligned with business outcomes. Collaboration needs to be mandatory.

Culture is crucial. A suboptimal culture will hinder the implementation of the frameworks and advice in this book and obstruct your attempts to accelerate value from data analytics. Before starting any data analytics initiative, assess your company's current behaviours, values and beliefs, and identify what needs to change to realise value. Your teams can then drive inter-ventions as part of these initiatives to increase your chances of success.

Consider these cultural models to improve your com-pany's culture, especially around data, if you do not already use a formal culture management model:

- The Competing Values Framework[31]

- Denison Model of Organizational Culture[32]

- Hall's Iceberg Model[33]

- McKinsey 7s Framework[34]

Common pitfalls and how to avoid them

Hiring sub-par data engineers is a common point of failure in data analytics functions. Business leaders may save 20% on salary, but this often leads to millions in wasted costs. It can even result in a data warehouse rebuild due to the mess created. Pay attention to these key hires and consider consulting support to select the right people. Your success depends on the quality of the people you appoint.

People costs are usually the highest cost component of a data analytics function and need to be prioritised. These costs do not follow a simple principle of *spend more, get more; spend less, get less*. For example, spending $10,000 to realise $100,000 in value might be effective. Spending $8,000 instead to save some money could result in losing $50,000 due to cleanup costs. Investing less than necessary can cause more damage than not investing; it might be better not to invest at all if proper expenditure is not possible.

Pitfalls often occur with deep technical skills in your data analytics function. When in doubt, seek advice. The cost savings and reduced pain will be worth the extra investment.

Tips for sourcing talent

To attract high-calibre staff, implement these strategies:

1. Choose your data analytics leader carefully with the help of an experienced data strategy consultant.

2. Hire the best data experts you can afford, focusing on areas where you own the algorithm.

3. Recognise that people are crucial in data analytics-led initiatives and must be aligned across functions for success.

4. Integrate data value culture into your company values and celebrate when new data skills and capabilities are developed.

5. Make data value culture a priority; identify and address areas of cultural weakness and address them.

6. Showcase your company's strong data value-driven culture, highlighting your commitment to data analytics-driven decision-making and projects.

7. Invest strategically in modern tools and technologies.

8. Offer competitive compensation and benefits.

9. Focus on skills development and learning programmes.

10. Consider the challenges of the data analytics function and provide the support it needs.

Final thoughts on people and building a strong data value culture

Attracting, enabling and retaining the right data professionals is key to extracting value from your data. Like refining water to make it drinkable, these critical team members can turn your raw, unrefined data into insights that can drive value-generating decisions.

As a leader, your role is to assemble the best players and ensure they have the environment, support and direction they need to succeed. This chapter has provided you with the STACKER+DVC framework – a tool to help you structure your teams effectively, foster a culture of continuous learning, and safeguard against key-person dependencies.

By investing in the right people and building a culture that values data analytics-driven decision-making, you can navigate the complexities of managing in-demand talent and avoid the common pitfalls that could derail your efforts. This approach will set the stage for your company to not only survive but thrive in a data-driven world.

In the next chapter we will explore the frameworks that will help you deliver on the promises of your data strategy. Just as a conductor relies on a well-composed score to guide the orchestra, you need robust frameworks to guide the implementation and delivery of your data analytics-led initiatives. Let's keep building on our strong foundations and continue our journey to data analytics-driven success.

Key chapter takeaways

- Talent management is crucial for turning raw data into valuable insights, making your data analytics function a strategic asset.

- People and culture are deeply interconnected and must be managed as one ecosystem to drive sustained success in data analytics-led initiatives.

- A well-defined structure within your data analytics function is essential to optimise execution, ensuring that the team operates harmoniously and efficiently to unlock valuable insights.

- Continuous training is fundamental for success. It ensures that your data team remains agile, up to date with relevant skills and aligned with business objectives.

- Attracting and retaining top data analytics talent is vital. These professionals are the key to transforming raw data into valuable insights that drive strategic decisions and innovation.

- Capacitating your data analytics teams with adequate people and support is vital to managing workload, avoiding burnout and ensuring consistent value generation.

- Mitigating key-person dependency risks through cross-training, documentation and proactive talent management is essential to maintaining resilience and continuity in your data analytics function.

- A robust data value culture, where data is trusted, accessible and used to drive decision-making, is critical for realising value from data analytics-led initiatives.

A NOTE FOR DIVISIONAL AND SUBSIDIARY LEADERS

You face unique challenges in implementing the people and data value culture concepts from this chapter within your broader corporate framework.

A careful approach to adapting the STACKER+DVC framework is required to balance centralised corporate policies with the specific needs of your division. Additional justifications may be required to obtain approvals from your corporate office.

Resource constraints may limit your ability to fully implement every aspect of the framework, so it is important to prioritise investments in people and culture that will have the most significant impact. Additionally, managing key-person dependency within smaller teams requires special care.

Establishing a unified data value culture across diverse business functions or regions in larger groups requires strategic focus to reap the benefits.

By paying specific attention to addressing these challenges, you can effectively deliver your division's data analytics-led initiatives, leading the charge with local successes while contributing to the goals of the broader group.

SIX

Approach To Delivering Insights – The SCRAPPAD, DRIVER And DATABRIDGE Frameworks

I n today's complex business landscape, data is a cornerstone of success. Insightful decisions can be game-changing, but we are inundated with information, and business leaders often find themselves overwhelmed. They might well find themselves asking:

- Which data is valuable?

- What can be ignored?

- What does this data mean?

- What data do I need to run my business?

The true challenge lies not in the amount of data collected but in the ability to harness its power to produce insights that can drive value. This potential value is unquestionable when algorithms operate in harmony to unveil insights that unlock hidden opportunities, uncover risks and enable strategic foresight.

This chapter establishes a standard delivery model for data analytics solutions, going beyond guiding principles to ensure continuity, manage stakeholder expectations, and focus the team on the most important initiatives to maximise value.

Why should you, as a business leader, read this chapter? Think of data analytics as the human anatomy. Just as you do not need to be a doctor to understand how your body functions – you know the basic functions of your eyes, heart, lungs, hands and feet – a degree in data is not required to understand the core processes of your data analytics function. A basic understanding of your anatomy enables you to operate the various parts together to achieve outcomes. Similarly, understanding the key components of your data analytics function will empower you to drive value without needing to be an expert.

Where margins for error are narrow and stakes high, leveraging the full potential of your data is not only an advantage – it is imperative. We will demonstrate that a formal approach to data analytics delivery is no longer a choice but rather a cornerstone for sustainable success.

CASE STUDY: Framework-based success –
journey to a trillion-dollar valuation

Apple's rise to a trillion-dollar valuation was far from
easy. By the late 1990s, the company was in serious
decline and risked obscurity, with revenue plummeting
from $11 billion in 1995 to $5.9 billion in 1998, its
lowest point in that decade.[35]

In 1997 Steve Jobs returned as interim CEO, facing a
seemingly insurmountable challenge, with the share
price at $0.16 per share, down from $0.50 in 1991.[36]
Apple was on the brink of collapse.

Jobs, a true visionary, had realised after his earlier
departure from Apple that his strength was not in
execution. He needed someone to fill that gap. In March
1998 Jobs appointed Tim Cook as senior vice president
of worldwide operations.[37] Apple was near bankruptcy,
with low employee morale. Cook, with his procurement
expertise and affinity for leveraging robust frameworks,
complemented Jobs' vision, making them an ideal team.

Jobs and Cook set about implementing clear frameworks
to guide Apple's recovery.[38] They defined specific roles
and responsibilities across teams, ensuring everyone
understood their contribution to profitability – whether
it was the design team creating innovative products,
the engineering team bringing those ideas to life, or the
marketing team taking the products to market.

This approach was not an overnight success. Revenue
fell to $5.4 billion in 2001, but Jobs focused on
the long game. By 2012 – just eleven years later –
Apple's revenue had soared to $157 billion[39], and

the share price had climbed to over $16 per share[40], demonstrating the lasting impact of his leadership.

Much of Apple's turnaround success was due to the clear frameworks and handover points established by Cook, leveraging his supply chain expertise. By aligning every team's responsibilities, Jobs and Cook drove Apple to unprecedented profitability – a remarkable success story.

This chapter draws parallels to Apple's success by focusing on the power of defined, interlinked frameworks to coordinate efforts and achieve success in complex environments.

The perils of missing frameworks

Driving value through data analytics hinges on cost-effectively producing consolidated and reliable data, which requires the adoption of frameworks and coordinated efforts across various data disciplines. The complexity of a typical company's data environment means that addressing one aspect in isolation can lead to long-term negative impacts, as illustrated by the call centre agent example in Chapter Five. Often, the consequences of missing frameworks and processes only become apparent further downstream in unrelated areas.

This interdependence between business, data and IT capabilities is what formal enterprise architecture is designed to manage. Even though it is notoriously difficult to directly quantify the value of enterprise architecture, it remains a critical link in the data analytics value chain, ensuring that all elements work together effectively to drive value.

We have helped numerous companies recover from the fallout of missing frameworks. The symptoms, all producing untrustworthy results, are always the same:

- A lack of delivery of value-driving insights
- Ad hoc processes
- Unreliable data platforms

Above all, we are consistently struck by the amount of unnecessary rework caused by poorly designed architecture. Each new requirement forces these teams to start from scratch, leading to inefficiencies and wasted effort. It is like the recent improvements made to a Formula 1 circuit, where changes were needed for more excitement and overtaking. Instead of tearing down the entire track and starting over, the organisers made targeted adjustments, enhancing what was already in place.[41] Similarly, in data analytics, the goal is to continue building on existing structures rather than constantly rebuilding from the ground up.

These undesirable outcomes often lead to shadow data analytics functions, increasing risk and governance challenges. Without formal frameworks, performance suffers, costs rise and revenue may be lost. Failing to properly plan your approach is equivalent to planning to fail in implementation.

Inadequate data consolidation hampers the adoption of cutting-edge technologies like AI. Most companies are not ready to fully leverage these technologies until they establish foundational structures for the cost-effective production of reliable data for analytics. As the rigidity of a race car enables it to corner faster, the more structured your approach, the more agile you are, and the more ready you will be to implement powerful new technologies with relative ease.

Building data analytics solutions – a wolf in sheep's clothing

At the start, a data analytics journey seems straightforward: collect data, consolidate it and produce insights. Companies often begin by hiring data analysts without considering the need for scalability.

As the data analytics team delivers initial results, stakeholder demand increases. They soon request daily insights, prompting the need for automation – a step that should have been anticipated.

A data engineer is brought in to automate processes, and soon the team is building and automating new solutions. However, as the environment grows more complex, rework and maintenance escalate.

Time passes, and the team has grown significantly, delivering hundreds of solutions but still operating haphazardly. Leadership questions the value generated versus the escalating costs, as the demand for more team members continues without clear justification.

This is when we get called to consult with the company's leadership, who are at their wits' end. Costs are out of control, value is questionable, and they are concerned about falling behind.

The following points summarise our usual findings in these situations. They illustrate why continuing without defined frameworks is a costly mistake.

1. Starting projects without clear business requirements leads to costly rework, easily doubling delivery costs and hindering value realisation.

2. Where automation should be used, manual processes dominate, often leading to build costs five times higher than necessary. The common mistake is that automation requires standardisation, which is frequently missing due to the absence of frameworks.

3. Maintenance consumes up to 50% of the team's capacity, leaving less time for value generation. Without standardisation and automation, rising complexity leads to increasing maintenance costs, outstripping any value generated.

4. Uncoordinated planning, data collection, consolidation and cleansing processes force data scientists to spend up to 80% of their time on these tasks rather than developing value-driving solutions. The absence of automation increases risk and complexity and, therefore, cost.

5. Poorly optimised code leads to slow, unreliable data platforms and can result in data platform costs being up to 30% higher than necessary.

6. A lack of formal standards leads to unsupportable solutions when team members leave, often requiring costly and time-consuming rebuilds.

7. Data quality issues are not addressed at the source but in analytics processes, slowing down delivery, and burdening the analytics function and data platform. Poor data quality drives up costs, with the 1:10:100 rule showing that prevention is far cheaper than correction, and doing nothing is 100 times more costly than prevention.[42]

8. Routine changes such as integrating new applications or upgrading systems cause major disruptions, due to weak data analytics frameworks and architecture.

9. Projects to migrate data platforms incur high build costs and can cause months of disruption, leaving companies stuck on legacy platforms. Unable to justify the investment and downtime, companies often run modern and legacy platforms in parallel, driving up costs, which places value realisation beyond reach.

10. Executives often become frustrated with delays in value delivery. They know that each delay results in lost value, but they lack the confidence or experience to implement necessary changes.

Teams experiencing these issues often lack awareness of the severity of the setbacks. They have no reference point for what 'good' looks like. They are stuck with their second-rate approach, despite constantly fighting to keep their heads above water, trying to manage 'difficult stakeholders' and 'impossible expectations'. They are constantly at loggerheads with each other and their stakeholders – an unpleasant cycle of attack and defence leading to further inefficiency and wasted effort.

The greatest cost is the loss of leadership confidence, causing hesitance to invest further in data analytics-led initiatives. This hesitance incurs a high opportunity cost and prevents the company from building a competitive advantage.

These issues can be addressed with a robust approach to delivering insights, as we will explore next.

Unleashing strategic advantage with a robust approach

A strategic approach to delivering value-driving insights can significantly reduce costs, addressing all the challenges highlighted above. With a well-defined framework, maintenance costs can be reduced from up to 50% to below 10% of a team's capacity, no matter the complexity or volume of solutions.

This efficiency frees highly skilled and sought-after data scientists to focus on high-impact solutions instead of routine tasks. Standardised optimisation patterns help control platform costs, and our approach reduces the need for heavy investments during application integrations and upgrades. Automating critical data consolidation eases platform migrations, allowing simplified transitions to more advanced technologies.

A robust approach builds leadership confidence and empowers you and your team to take bold steps towards innovation and growth. Every improvement you make sets the stage for long-term success and competitive advantage. This positive momentum leads to further investment, creating a positive feedback loop that enables the company to leverage its most valuable asset – data – to achieve exceptional results.

Delivering valuable insights through strategic frameworks

This approach comprises three frameworks, each targeting a specific area of the data analytics solution delivery process. As demonstrated by Steve Jobs at Apple, clear frameworks, defined roles and smooth handovers between sub-functions are crucial for success.

The three frameworks introduced in this chapter are:

1. SCRAPPAD for delivery management

2. DRIVER for data analytics project delivery

3. DATABRIDGE for data architecture and engineering

We will focus on key aspects of each framework that are relevant to business leaders, particularly in enforcing standards and compliance. Understanding these components will help you drive efficiency and optimisation, benefiting your teams through your leadership in driving value realisation.

These interconnected frameworks ensure an operationally sound data analytics value chain. The delivery management capability gathers, prioritises and hands over demand to the data analytics delivery function, which then relies on data architecture and engineering for technical requirements. After project completion, responsibility returns to delivery management for change and release coordination.

Refer to the diagram below to see how these frameworks interconnect, using it as a guide throughout this chapter.

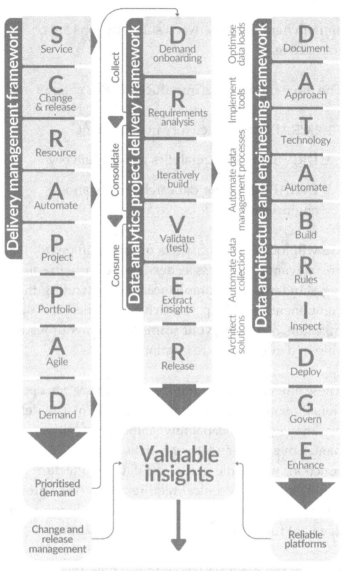

Delivery management framework

S	Service
C	Change & release
R	Resource
A	Automate
P	Project
P	Portfolio
A	Agile
D	Demand

Collect
Consolidate
Consume

Data analytics project delivery framework

D	Demand onboarding
R	Requirements analysis
I	Iteratively build
V	Validate (test)
E	Extract insights
R	Release

Optimise data loads
Implement tools
Automate data management processes
Automate data collection
Architect solutions

Data architecture and engineering framework

D	Document
A	Approach
T	Technology
A	Automate
B	Build
R	Rules
I	Inspect
D	Deploy
G	Govern
E	Enhance

Prioritised demand

Change and release management

Valuable insights

Reliable platforms

Integrate insights to drive value
Embed insights in business processes and applications

Data value architect

The connected frameworks for the approach to delivering insights

The SCRAPPAD framework for delivery management

The CEO wants a report, the sales team needs insights, marketing needs campaign stats, and one of the dashboards did not refresh correctly because the data platform crashed. Welcome to a typical Monday morning for a data analytics function.

Data analytics teams often struggle with competing demands. They face an identity crisis, being seen as both technical teams and as business consultants. This confusion leads to execution without thought or justification. Where focus is required, context switching is the norm, which limits value creation.

While frameworks like ITIL 4, COBIT, PMP and Agile are valuable, they aren't tailored for data analytics delivery. They often cause unnecessary overhead, especially in run-of-the-mill smaller projects and ad hoc tasks.

The SCRAPPAD framework combines best practices into a tailored approach, enabling data analytics teams to manage diverse demands and improve focus and productivity, thereby unlocking capacity for innovation and enhancing value delivery.

The SCRAPPAD framework draws from three of the industry-standard frameworks:

- **Service management (ITIL 4)** – For service cataloguing and service-level agreements in data analytics delivery

- **Project management (PMP)** – For project governance and executive awareness

- **Task management (Agile)** – For accelerating time-to-value

The Agile Manifesto is one of the first examples of a whole industry coming together to build something new and establish a standard. This was a pivotal moment for software development. We consider Agile a critical component of the RAPPID Value Cycle as it complements the requirement for phased delivery.

SCRAPPAD incorporates several interconnected concepts, designed to help data analytics teams focus and manage stakeholder expectations effectively. As a business leader, understanding the impact of these components on value realisation is key. The acronym stands for (numbered order in parenthesis):

- **S**ervice management (1)

- **C**hange and release management (6)

- **R**esource management (3)

- **A**gile task management (8)

- **P**roject management (4)

- **P**ortfolio management (7)

- Automation of delivery management (5)

- Demand management (2)

The order of explanation of each element below, differs from the order of the SCRAPPAD acronym. This is to enable better understanding of the SCRAPPAD framework.

1. Service management

The service catalogue defines and categorises the services offered by the data analytics function (e.g., strategic projects, ad hoc requests, etc), helping manage stakeholder expectations through clear service levels and timelines. This promotes accountability and enhances the robustness of data analytics solutions.

2. Demand management

Demand management includes four components:

- **Demand capture.** This needs to be centralised, ongoing and automated, initially feeding from the demand consolidation process explained in Chapter Three. The initial consolidated list of value-generating initiatives is the starting point for demand capture, and it is expanded through the ongoing collection of new demand. The demand capture process is a single point of entry for all demand, ensuring focused delivery by eliminating ungoverned channels, like direct messages to data engineers. Key data gathered during demand capture includes service categorisation, business priority, and alignment with strategic objectives.

- **Demand clarification.** This relies on the value forecasting approach explained in Chapter Three, and on generating the potential result of value extraction (PROVE), discussed in Chapter Four. These processes focus on creating business cases that forecast determinate value for high-impact value-generating initiatives necessary for effective prioritisation of demand. These business cases must include the investments required beyond data analytics capabilities, which must include business process changes, IT application updates, employee training, etc, to ensure that determinate value is realised.

- **Demand prioritisation.** This should follow a value-driven framework (e.g., RICE, Kano, MoSCoW), relying on the business cases developed in demand clarification.

- **Demand reporting.** This takes place through distribution of updates and in a regular cadence of reporting sessions to keep stakeholders informed, manage their expectations and build their confidence in the delivery process. This transparency ensures you have a clear idea of what will be required to address the demand and whether requirements for additional investments in people, platforms, etc, are justified.

3. Resource management

Effective capacity planning and resource scheduling are key to ensuring focused delivery of critical business requirements.

4. Project management

Standardised project planning templates ensure consistent delivery timelines and quality, with governance processes and regular reporting sessions to keep stakeholders informed.

5. Automation of delivery management

Automation of demand capture, classification, prioritisation and project management reduces rework and enforces standards, creating a consistent data analytics function.

6. Change and release management

It is important to define 'done' to ensure projects are formally closed out and releases are managed smoothly.

Remember that as part of change management, stakeholders must be supported in adopting the new structured approach for demand management.

7. Portfolio management

This provides stakeholders with a high-level over-view of data analytics delivery to enable them to prioritise business support efforts and sustain value realisation.

8. Agile task management

Task allocation and tracking ensure accountabil-ity and adaptability, giving leaders confidence in focused and flexible delivery. They also provide con-fidence in driving changes in direction when busi-ness priorities shift.

Handover from SCRAPPAD to DRIVER

As illustrated in the figure above, the SCRAPPAD delivery management framework primarily produces prioritised demand. Essentially, this is a prioritised list of data analytics projects that need to be handed over for execution, which is managed through the DRIVER data analytics project delivery framework. The key handover component is *demand onboarding* informa-tion (the first component of the DRIVER framework), which enables accelerated requirement analysis and solution architecture in the DRIVER processes.

The DRIVER framework for data analytics project delivery

At the start of a data analytics project, the requestor of a requirement rarely has a comprehensive vision of the final solution. Projects can become direction-less without a clear approach, leading to delays and dissatisfaction. This lack of clarity hampers accurate timeline forecasting and value realisation.

Adopting a pure agile methodology might seem like a solution, but it introduces uncertainty in costs and timelines, often leading to extended experimentation without clear outcomes. This approach can result in proof of concept (POC) purgatory, where projects lose direction and fail to deliver value by not proceeding beyond the POC state – a disappointing outcome for projects with high potential for value creation.

The key to setting a fixed timeline in data analytics delivery is thorough upfront analysis. By addressing all critical questions early, you clarify the end state, reduce uncertainty, and accurately estimate resources and timelines, thereby ensuring commitments to budget and delivery are met.

Standardising the delivery approach significantly improves estimation accuracy. Each project may seem unique, which is what your data engineers will argue as they seek creative ways to solve problems that appear in every project. However, value comes from adhering to established frameworks, which are essential for consistency in budgeting and time-lines. Problem-solving is important, but it must occur within predefined parameters to avoid key-person dependencies, unreliable solutions and costly rework. It is imperative for data engineers to embrace structured frameworks, thereby fostering confidence in your data analytics journey.

The DRIVER framework accelerates delivery, enhances value and improves the reliability of data analytics solutions, offering predictability in timelines. Value realisation from data analytics-led initiatives relies strongly on successfully adopting the DRIVER framework. As a leader, your support is crucial for maximising its value creation potential.

Remember that, when operating without a guiding framework, your teams may feel frustrated and unrecognised, struggling with demanding stakeholders. It is difficult for them to see the sun shining nearby while they are stuck in the eye of the storm. You can support them by considering the following framework components to enhance their efforts and drive value through your data analytics journey.

DRIVER stands for:

1. **D**emand onboarding

2. **R**equirements analysis

3. **I**teratively build

4. Validate (test)

5. Extract insights

6. Release

1. Demand onboarding

This stage involves transitioning from the SCRAPPAD framework, using the demand information gathered to estimate delivery effort, timelines and a high-level solution architecture.

Clarity of purpose is essential for data analytics teams. As a business leader, you must ensure the team understands the problem they are solving, its impact on the company, and the value it will generate. This clarity aligns efforts with company priorities and removes barriers to value creation.

2. Requirements analysis

Clearly defining requirements is critical. Business leaders are typically good at the critical thinking required to generate robust requirements, but they tend to take the easy way out and push the responsibility to the data analytics function to figure out what they need to do. This never works well.

Stakeholders must actively engage in this process rather than leave it to the data analytics team. A structured approach ensures the team understands what is needed and aligns their efforts with business goals.

Begin by defining clear business objectives and then identifying key questions that will guide your analytics team towards value realisation. Focus on the most critical information required to address the opportunity or pain point so your data analytics function has a foundation from which to gather further information. You can use these questions as a guide:

- What problems/opportunities exist that need to be addressed?

- Do you have a possible solution, or do you expect your data analytics function to help you identify possible solutions?

- Do you know what decisions you want to make once you gain access to the insights you seek?

- Is the company ready to deal with the output of the insights you expect and can you use them to realise determinate value?

- Are any additional actions, mandates, funding, etc, required to take action on the insights you have gathered to realise value?

This non-exhaustive list of considerations will help streamline the requirements analysis process, avoiding analysis paralysis, and ensuring your analytics team remains focused and effective. The relevant business stakeholder must sign off requirements before proceeding to the build phase.

3. Iteratively build

This stage involves executing the priorities and requirements identified in demand onboarding and requirements analysis. It follows an agile-style delivery approach, with a recommended 10% flexibility to accommodate minor adjustments without causing significant disruption. The build process includes several key steps:

- **Collect:** Establish processes to gather data from source applications and datasets into a landing area, with automated refresh schedules. Ensure monitoring is in place at every step to maintain data consistency. If inconsistencies arise, it may indicate a lack of proper monitoring, which needs to be addressed.

- **Consolidate:** Combine and match data in a consolidation layer for consumption, focusing strictly on the agreed scope. Avoid manual development to reduce costs, maintenance and key-person dependencies, and ensure the approach adopted allows for easy scaling.

- **Consume:** Develop solution components – such as reports, dashboards and analytics models – that align with the agreed requirements and scope, and that drive actionable business outcomes.

- **Measure value:** Incorporate value measurement and reporting into analytics solutions, focusing on agreed metrics and ensuring clarity on the value delivered.

- **Publish data trust components:** Ensure transparency by publishing components that build trust in analytics results. These include definitions, methods, sources and data quality metrics. This step is crucial for maintaining trust in data analytics results and should be mandatory. In Chapter Eight, we explore these concepts in more detail.

4. Validate (test)

Testing serves three purposes:

- Verifying accuracy of results

- Documenting results for UAT

- Reusing tests for automated monitoring

Your team should be able to confirm that the solution meets the requirements and performs as expected.

5. Extract insights

Critical thinking is essential here. Ensure that the insights delivered align with the business questions identified earlier. If not, work with the team to iterate and refine to extract the required insights. Embedding these insights into business applications and processes is crucial for extracting value, which will be facilitated by the role introduced in Chapter Nine.

6. Release

If your company is new to data analytics-driven decision-making, this step will require special care. The team needs to collaborate closely with the business to ensure integration of the insights into processes. Support from leadership is crucial to monitor and report on usage, with value realised being the ultimate measure of success. Once again, embedding insights into the business is critical for value realisation.

DRIVER handover back to SCRAPPAD

The handover back to SCRAPPAD focuses on tracking *change and release* activities within demand management. These important activities are often forgotten, leading to valuable data analytics solutions ending on the rubbish dump because teams fail to take the care required to embed solutions in business processes. Therefore, applying project management over the change and release activities is crucial for success, and these activities must be standardised in your delivery management processes.

Traditionally, keys to success in change management would typically involve improving a report or dashboard, and training a user how to use the report or dashboard. However, experience has taught us that properly embedded solutions are more naturally adopted because they enhance value delivery by optimising business processes through insights. Users don't want dashboards that add an extra step in their process. They want embedded insights to make their processes more efficient and their decisions more accurate.

Handover from DRIVER to DATABRIDGE

The handover from DRIVER to DATABRIDGE involves areas where data analysts need deeper technical support from data architects and engineers. Specific needs are identified during the execution of DRIVER processes, specifically *requirements analysis*. A data analyst, for example, will identify that a new tool is required to implement a solution. The request is sent to the data architecture and engineering team to implement the tool, which becomes a dependency for the delivery of the solution. The DRIVER delivery processes are placed on hold at the *iterative build* stage until the relevant tool is implemented through the DATABRIDGE processes.

Further technical requirements, like for data load optimisation, are sometimes only identified during the *iterative build* stage, requiring immediate support from a data engineer to move the project forward.

While this handover focuses on technical aspects, ensuring smooth handover and clear mandates is crucial for efficiency, particularly in automating routine tasks. Most of your opportunities to create efficiencies lie in enabling data engineers to automate routine activities in data analytics delivery.

Key handover points:

1. **Architect solutions:** Non-standard solutions require data architects to design and develop the required architecture.

2. **Automate data collection:** Some data collection processes need technical expertise, like API connections.

3. **Automate data management processes:** Automating intensive manual data management processes, such as mastering customer records or applying complex data quality rules, is crucial.

4. **Implement tools:** Specific tools may be needed for certain analytics solutions.

5. **Optimise data loads:** Data analysts may need technical support from data platform engineers for building and optimising complex data loading and processing tasks.

The DATABRIDGE framework for data architecture and engineering

Data architects and data engineers must follow a structured framework to ensure their work consistently delivers value. The frameworks discussed in this chapter are designed to provide that essential structure and focus.

Allowing technical teams to develop solutions based on intuition alone leads to tangled, unmanageable systems that require extensive maintenance and costly recovery efforts. Without a formal framework, while fighting technical debt,* technical teams tend to create more technical debt. Following a defined framework for data architecture and engineering builds a robust data analytics environment underpinned by reliability, resilience and supportability.

The DATABRIDGE framework for data architecture and engineering includes the following key components:

---

* Technical debt: When technical teams prioritise convenient shortcuts that produce faster results over carefully planned, long-term solutions, the outcome is inevitably unfavourable, but the impact is only felt months or years later, often after the responsible individuals have moved on. Technical debt refers to the liability caused by effort required to rework technical solutions to address the negative impacts. In many cases, fixes are too expensive to even consider addressing, especially when solution-stacking has occurred (when multiple solutions are built on top of a workaround or shortcut). The effect on a company can be catastrophic, as maintenance costs start to outstrip the value generated by solutions. Often the only viable outcome is to rip and replace.

1. Document

2. Approach

3. Technology

4. Automate

5. Build in phases

6. Rules and standards

7. Inspect

8. Deploy

9. Govern

10. Enhance

1. Document

Confidence in sustainable delivery requires solutions to be well documented, meaning they are easy to audit, support and improve. Adequate documentation is crucial for preventing key-person dependencies.

2. Approach

A best practice approach needs to be adopted – through frameworks like Data Vault, DataOps, Data Fabric, etc – to ensure reliability and reduce key-person dependency. Review the frameworks' strategies and delivery tracking methods to validate your teams' use of the frameworks.

3. Technology

You can save costs and eliminate duplication of functionality by ensuring that technology platforms are rationalised and cost-optimised, involving your CIO and architecture teams to ensure that technology is adequately utilised. Keep your technology use in check, ensuring alignment with business and IT strategies.

4. Automate

Focusing on automation and configurability will accelerate delivery and reduce costs. The principle is to 'build once, use many times'. This requires more foresight and careful thought than simply building.

The prerequisite for automation is standardisation, which is enabled by implementing a best-practice approach. Measure your teams' efficiency in creating value and ensure they follow sustainable practices.

5. Build in phases

Manage expectations, insisting that delivery is incremental. Otherwise, the team will go away and try to solve everything simultaneously, which is not recommended. Remember that they are trying to impress you as the stakeholder – to their own detriment and to yours. Work with your delivery management team to set realistic timelines and understand the value at each stage, to avoid placing unnecessary pressure on the team.

6. Rules and standards

Streamline resource allocation and improve efficiency with defined rules and standards, allowing quick transitions between tasks and projects. These guardrails accelerate delivery and reduce maintenance.

7. Inspect (monitor)

Ensure that solutions are monitored for the reliability of analytics outputs and value creation. Stakeholders need to be informed of any issues as they arise. Early notifications prevent surprises, like last-minute dashboard updates before crucial meetings.

8. Deploy

Ensure stable deployments by collaborating with IT teams and establishing processes that avoid disruptions to business-critical solutions.

9. Govern

Ensure high-quality solutions by vetting them with data governance teams, IT and relevant stakeholders.

Use internal audit to enforce governance and hold teams accountable for compliance, which can otherwise often be placed on the back burner in favour of getting the job done.

10. Enhance

We have never seen a solution deliver to its full potential without some revision and improvement. Regularly review and enhance solutions to ensure they improve. Focus on improving value realisation as the main objective, guided by the 'Improve value' approach from Chapter Three.

Cultural impact on data analytics approach

Deeply ingrained cultural values can render formal approaches irrelevant. The success of a data analytics journey depends on a company's receptiveness to change. Cultures of accountability, transparency and collaboration enable faster and higher-quality insights.

A culture that tolerates individual work, silos and rigidity may resist positive change, viewing frameworks as disruptive. This can lead to workarounds, with processes prioritised over achieving goals, and even passive resistance or sabotage.

To overcome cultural challenges, identify their root cause, which is often found in leadership style. For example, leaders that focus on self-promotion foster resistance to change, while those prioritising accountability and collaboration create an environment open to improvement.

Building a world-class data analytics delivery approach starts with evaluating your leadership culture. Without addressing cultural impact, even the best frameworks will fall short.

Common pitfalls and how to avoid them

Data analytics journeys inevitably expose companies to the pervasive influence of hype. This phenomenon is often instigated by software vendors vying for prominence in a competitive landscape. In their quest for market share, these vendors are inclined to exaggerate the capabilities of their products, potentially leading business leaders astray. It is crucial to recognise:

- The mere capability of a tool to execute tasks does not automatically translate to value.

- A tool's features do not automatically align it with the company's strategic objectives or operational needs.

Companies should prioritise a principled and process-driven approach rather than succumbing to the attraction of technology trends. This entails meticulously outlining the guiding principles and frameworks that underpin data analytics projects before selecting the appropriate technology solutions to support these frameworks.

CASE STUDY: Automate – build once, deliver many

Darren Finkelstein worked under the inspirational leadership of Steve Jobs during Apple's strategic transformation period between 1997 and 2002, as manager of commercial markets for Australia. In our interview with Darren, he recalled that a guiding principle Steve Jobs applied was 'build once, deliver many.' This philosophy directed creators to produce high-quality multimedia content that could easily adapt to different channels, from print media to online advertising. Besides streamlining the production process by removing rework, this genius approach also amplified the reach and impact of the content, enabling creators to do more with less, which led to massive savings in content production costs. This ethos became a mantra that drove efficiency and creative excellence, both fundamental to Apple's renown.

This principle applies equally to the world of data architecture and engineering, and drives similar impact. Focusing on building automation and configurability requires more foresight and experience than simply building. This is the mark of a data engineering capability that can support a value-generating data analytics journey with reliable platforms that will scale as the business grows, and adapt easily to inevitable change. Automation accelerates delivery pace and reduces build and maintenance costs.

The foundation for automation is standardisation, which is enabled by implementing a best-practice approach. Direct your teams to follow standardised processes, which will improve their ability to create value.

Final thoughts: Leveraging frameworks for delivering insights

Just as Steve Jobs orchestrated Apple's turnaround by meticulously defining roles, responsibilities and handover points, your company's success in data analytics hinges on adopting a structured, framework-driven approach. Think of your data analytics function as the engine of a finely tuned race car. Without the right structure, even the most powerful engine will struggle on the track, leading to costly maintenance and lost opportunities. When frameworks like SCRAPPAD, DRIVER and DATABRIDGE are interconnected and work in harmony, they keep your engine running smoothly, accelerating value delivery and ensuring sustained performance.

This chapter has laid the groundwork for understanding how these frameworks can transform your data analytics journey from a disjointed effort into a well-oiled machine. By embracing these structured approaches, you will reduce the costs of inefficiency and rework and position your company to leverage data as a true competitive advantage.

As you move forward, these frameworks are your tools for creating a culture of accountability, collaboration and continuous improvement. With these tools in hand, you have the power to lead your company to new heights, unlocking the full potential of your data and driving impactful, lasting change.

In the next chapter we will dive into what is often the most significant cost burden of any data analytics journey: the data platform. We will explore strategies to manage and reduce these costs, ensuring that your platform is an investment that propels your company forward. Just as the frameworks discussed here provide structure, the right approach to your data platform will provide the foundation for future success. Stay with us as we build on these ideas and continue to chart your path to data analytics-driven excellence.

Key chapter takeaways

- A formal, structured approach to data analytics, using clear frameworks and defined handover points, is essential for reducing costs, improving efficiency and ensuring sustainable value creation.

- Companies without structured approaches may fall into inefficiency, incur excessive maintenance costs and miss opportunities, leading to a loss of leadership confidence and potential competitive disadvantage.

- Investing early in scalable and automated processes will prevent costly rework. This will allow your data analytics team to focus on generating high-impact insights rather than routine tasks.

- The SCRAPPAD, DRIVER and DATABRIDGE frameworks provide a comprehensive delivery model that addresses demand management, project delivery, data architecture and data engineering, ensuring coordinated efforts across all aspects of data analytics.

- The SCRAPPAD framework standardises delivery and project management to create focus and manage stakeholder expectations.

- The DRIVER framework enhances data analytics project delivery by ensuring thorough upfront analysis, standardising the delivery approach and fostering predictability in timelines. Combined, these factors accelerate value creation and improve solution reliability.

- The DATABRIDGE framework focuses on structured data architecture and engineering, emphasising documentation, automation, and adherence to best practices. This will enable you to build a robust, reliable and cost-effective data analytics environment.

- A culture of accountability, transparency and collaboration is essential for successfully implementing data analytics frameworks, while resistance to change can undermine even the best strategies.

- Business leaders must avoid the allure of technology hype and instead focus on principles and processes to ensure that tools align with strategic objectives and drive real value.

A NOTE FOR DIVISIONAL AND SUBSIDIARY LEADERS

You may face challenges when implementing the frameworks discussed in this chapter. Limited autonomy within a larger corporate structure can make it difficult to fully adopt and apply the SCRAPPAD, DRIVER and DATABRIDGE frameworks to your specific needs. The success of these frameworks also depends heavily on cross-functional collaboration, which can be challenging to foster in environments where operations are siloed or shared corporate services do not prioritise your division's specific objectives.

Aligning these frameworks with both your local goals and the broader corporate strategy requires careful navigation. This is especially true when the corporate culture does not fully support the level of transparency, accountability and collaboration necessary for these frameworks to thrive. Lastly, integrating the necessary technology tools and platforms as outlined in the DATABRIDGE framework may prove difficult if corporate-standardised platforms or restrictions on adopting new technologies exist.

Awareness of these challenges can allow you to take proactive steps to align your division's initiatives with corporate expectations, foster cross-functional collaboration, and ensure that your efforts in data analytics continue to drive value within your specific context.

SEVEN

Platform Optimised For Value – The AC³ROS Framework

Today business leaders must combine technical and data expertise to create digital dexterity and truly drive impact. Many executives, driven by pressure and lacking data-confidence, rely on the excuse *I'm not a data geek* and then waste millions approving investments based on weak business cases.

Beyond technology and data, this chapter is about setting clear expectations for your technology investments and your data platform team. Understanding where value is lost and knowing how to address it can make you a powerful catalyst for improvement. This chapter will help you ask the right questions of your data and IT teams, enabling them to overcome obstacles to value realisation. This approach will elevate you as a highly impactful, data-confident leader.

This is likely the chapter that business leaders would most prefer to avoid. Press on, though – the principles we will cover for implementing and managing your data platform will address many value constraints in your data analytics journey. While this may seem challenging, mastering these principles will empower you to unlock tremendous value and set your business apart from the competition.

The timeless struggles of data platforms: Learning from the past

The story of the data platform is the same story seen so often. Your platform probably has some rich and interesting history, starting with a directive from your board to deploy it. You likely received promises of many bells and whistles, including a single view of the customer, real-time insights, big data, and data analytics-driven decision-making powered by AI. Soon after, though, you realised something was off.

You are not alone if you have questioned why you opted for a data platform and have little to show for the significant investment. Perhaps you feel uncertain about where things went wrong and lack the time or energy to fix it. Through countless demos and presentations, your team and vendors convinced you this platform was essential, only for the promised value to remain elusive.

Imagine a scenario where you move on, accepting that the platform serves a purpose, even if it is far from what was promised. Years later your team insists on an upgrade, and all those past frustrations come flooding back. Your patience quickly runs out, and you refuse to entertain jargon such as *true north* and *silver bullet* until the promised value is realised.

Your team is now stuck and frustrated with outdated technology. You eventually approve an upgrade to appease them, but your platform still lags behind those of your competitors, who keep innovating while you are fighting business-as-usual fires.

Your focus has shifted from driving value to cutting costs, and your decisions have become cautious. You have lost the conviction and confidence you are known for. Your impact on the company has diminished.

This is a common story. Most companies on a data platform journey experience this pain, while others manage to avoid it only because they have learnt from past mistakes.

This chapter introduces a framework to help you avoid these costly mistakes. We focus on value, not flashy features or vendor selection criteria. By prioritising value, you can equip your team with a strong mechanism to gain approval for necessary upgrades, giving them access to the latest technologies they require without having to rely on buzzwords or fanfare. Value realisation becomes the ultimate deciding factor.

By applying the framework in this chapter with the Data Income Statement introduced in Chapter Three, you can directly correlate platform costs with the value generated through data analytics. This will simplify technology investment decisions, accelerating the value you can drive through data analytics.

Before diving into the framework, we will clarify what we mean by *data platform.*

What is a data platform?

A data platform, usually also called a *data lake* or *data warehouse*, is not just about the technology used to centralise, store, and process data. Think of your data platform as the core enabler on which you build your data assets to derive value. Just as different types of companies require specific types of premises – such as a large flat area for a parking lot, a multistorey building for apartments, or a high-security facility for banks – your data platform must be tailored to the unique needs and objectives of your company.

The type of company you run dictates your data platform requirements, including the facilities and failovers necessary to ensure optimal operation and availability. Your data platform encompasses all the tools, applications, hardware, networking, infrastructure and cloud services (including SaaS platforms) that support your data analytics environment. This includes the full scope of your software and services tools, for:

- Storage

- Analytics workloads

- Data warehouse automation

- Data modelling

- Reporting

- Visualisation

- Dashboarding

- Deployment automation

- Orchestration

- Project and portfolio management

- Task management

- Workflow automation

Considering your data platform in this way makes it easier to determine what platform components you need to invest in. The right platform is not just a technical choice but also a strategic one, directly linked to your roadmap to generate value from your data. In the following sections, we will provide guidance to make these critical decisions, ensuring that your data platform is designed and implemented to fully support your objective to generate value.

The AC³ROS framework for platform optimisation

It is said that before a title fight in 1987, Mike Tyson was informed of how his opponent was convinced that he would take the title from Mike. It is claimed he gave a legendary response, which is also appropriate to data platform implementations: 'Everybody has plans until they get hit for the first time'.[43]

With data platform implementations, you will get punched so hard that you will not be able to think straight. It is crucial to prepare for the challenges before diving in.

The AC³ROS framework is where strategy meets reality. It helps business leaders focus on the most important components of technology when developing a data platform strategy. Use this framework during vendor presentations to not only take the punches thrown at you, but to also land a few of your own, bringing the focus onto what truly matters.

The following diagram introduces the AC³ROS framework for a platform optimised for value.

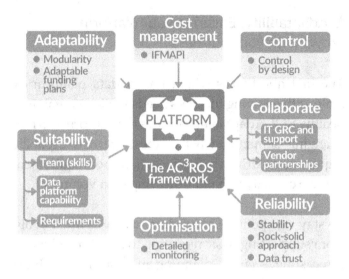

The AC³ROS framework for a platform optimised for value

The components of the AC³ROS framework are:

1. **A**daptability

2. **C**ost management

3. **C**ontrol

4. **C**ollaboration

5. **R**eliability

6. **O**ptimisation

7. **S**uitability

1. Adaptability: Ensuring your platform grows with your business

The first question is whether your data platform can scale with evolving business needs while maintaining a healthy ROI. Adaptability ensures the platform can meet changing demands, whether these are new capability requirements driven by business needs, or requirements to scale capacity to handle growing data volumes.

To stay competitive, your data platform must evolve from supporting basic reporting to enabling advanced forecasting, scenario planning and real-time analytics. For instance, real-time fraud analytics is now essential for relevance in financial services. An adaptable data platform is fundamental to keeping up.

Planning

Meticulous planning is essential for building an adaptable data platform, preventing bottlenecks that can lead to missed opportunities and unexpected costs.

For example, suppose you are building a revenue assurance model to understand your billing accuracy and recover lost revenue. At first you might only include a small percentage of available data in a POV. When the results show specific customer segments, products and billing rules affected by revenue leakage, you will want to scale up quickly and include all available data, to stop the leakage and recover revenue. Meticulous planning is required to avoid cost or performance constraints, or loss of potential value, at that point.

Beyond platform adaptability, your investment and funding approach must also be flexible. Quickly redirecting funding to scale successful initiatives accelerates value.

Modularity

Think about playing with Lego blocks. You build something and leave it for a few days, then return and add to the initial build quickly and easily. If you want to change something, you break apart a specific component and then rebuild it.

This describes a modular data platform – new technologies and capabilities can easily be added or modified without overhauling the entire system.

Scaling compute and storage

Compute (processing power) and storage (how much data can be stored) should scale automatically or with minimal effort. While most cloud platforms offer this, be wary of unexpected costs, but do not let previous experience discourage investment. Instead, build the capabilities to scale confidently – using the IFMAPI framework to track costs and ensure spending aligns with value generated.

255

Phasing delivery

Adopting a phased delivery approach for technology implementation increases adaptability (covered in the DATABRIDGE framework). By breaking down delivery into manageable phases, you will find that what once seemed overwhelming is not only achievable but also incredibly rewarding as you see tangible progress with each step. Avoid long-term projects by executing in short phases so that you can move faster than the pace of technological advancement. Otherwise, you may end up deploying solutions that are outdated before they go live.

If your data platform cannot adapt to growing business requirements, shadow data platforms may emerge as your company's leaders grow impatient. Leaders do not always have the luxury of waiting until the data platform is ready to take on their requirements. While shadow data platforms may offer short-term value, they increase long-term costs of and risks to data security and data governance. Adaptability is therefore essential.

2. Cost management: Cultivating a value-driven approach

Cost management and optimisation are major challenges for both cloud and on-premise data platforms. Questions about platform costs, how to reduce them, and the value generated are inevitable. To optimise spending, you may at some point need to consider alternative platform options, migration costs and the potential value of a migration.

First, let us explore cost optimisation approaches without migration.

Optimising cost without migrating your data platform

The most essential tool for managing data platform costs is a cost analysis that breaks down expenses per solution and incorporates the value generated, creating a net gain/loss view, as in the Data Income Statement in Chapter Three. Without this transparency, you will likely adopt a cost-reduction mindset due to uncertainty about value realisation, which stifles growth. With comprehensive cost analysis at hand, you can focus your optimisation efforts on areas of your data platform where value falls short. We like to call this *analytics on your analytics*. This insights-enabled approach fosters a value-driving mindset for your data platform.

Additionally, reduce platform costs by implementing a sound methodology for development (see Chapter Six). Support standardised approaches despite the required upfront investments and potential push-back from the team. Standardised approaches can reduce compute costs by embedding optimisation into the process.

Optimising cost through migrating to a cloud data platform

Migrating to a cloud-based platform or modernising your on-premise platform can reduce costs and provide a strategic advantage. In the early years of computing, companies had to pay exorbitant amounts to access computers, often through time-sharing models that allowed limited access via dedicated telephone lines. Over time, driven by IBM's dominance in mainframe computing, the model shifted to owning large-scale computing platforms. However, the landscape has evolved again with the advent of cloud computing, offering unprecedented flexibility and power.

With cloud adoption you gain the advantages of instant scalability, world-class security, embedded maintenance and access to the latest technology. You also avoid the burden of managing the platform or performing upgrades yourself. The operating expenses-based consumption model makes this more digestible for companies with limited capital, allowing you to focus investments on what indeed provides a strategic advantage. Owning a dedicated data platform server in your data centre is no longer a strategic advantage. Instead, cloud resources enable you to scale based on demand, access geographically distributed high availability, and simplify disaster recovery – all at a more affordable cost.

The principle of owning the algorithm supports this shift in focus. Your company's competitive edge needs to be driven by proprietary algorithms and data analytics-driven insights – the true drivers of value in a data-centric world – rather than physical servers and outdated technology. Migration to a cloud platform allows you to free up experts to invest in developing and refining these algorithms. Which would you prefer as your leadership's focus: managing infrastructure or leveraging opportunities for strategic revenue growth?

However, cloud migration is not without challenges. Costs can be complex and unexpected, and they can increase with usage. Careful monitoring of cost and value is essential.

Hybrid and multi-cloud deployments: A strategic stepping stone

Hybrid deployments offer a strategic way to begin your cloud journey, allowing you to focus on smaller, high-impact use cases before fully committing to cloud-based solutions. By starting with a hybrid approach, you can gradually migrate your data platform, ensuring that each step adds value and aligns with your overall strategy.

A multi-cloud approach provides even greater flexibility. By leveraging the strengths of multiple hyper-scalers, you can avoid vendor lock-in and optimise for best-of-breed solutions. For example, one provider may excel in reporting and analytics; while another offers superior traditional storage, compute capabilities and advanced AI services. A multi-cloud strategy allows you to select the best features from each provider, reducing risks associated with cost fluctuations. It can also ensure your data platform remains adaptable and aligned with your evolving business needs.

Optimising cloud costs through modularity and methodical migration

Consider modularity in your cloud data platform architecture as an essential cost-management technique. You want the ability to scale components of your data platform when required, instead of scaling the entire platform. Many modern cloud data platforms provide this type of benefit.

Avoid *lift and shift*** when migrating legacy processes, as they can increase costs. Instead, adapt legacy

---

** Lift and shift: This is a short way to describe the process of moving IT infrastructure from on-premise data centres into cloud data centres. We have consulted to many companies that had lost the cost benefit of cloud infrastructure migration because they had replicated their legacy platform processes in modern cloud technologies. These modern technologies require different approaches to what legacy teams are used to, and technical teams need to be open to adopting the new approaches to leverage the full benefits of the modern cloud technologies. In some cases, suboptimal approaches have incurred our clients more than five times the cost of optimal use. This is the reason lift and shift projects often have a negative perception in companies.

processes to leverage the new platform's features – otherwise, new platform costs will be higher than your current legacy platform. Your engineers may maintain that they can handle the platform migration themselves. If you are uncertain about this, consider involving platform providers to assess your team's technical capabilities. Ensure your team is trained and certified to avoid sub-optimal use of the new platform, which will increase cost.

Unmanaged costs will lead to unpleasant surprises, pulling you back into a cost-reduction mindset, which limits growth. View data platform costs as essential investments that yield returns. To adopt the mindset that these costs are essential for growth, build the capability to monitor costs against value generated.

3. Control: Platform governance, compliance and security

Regulatory requirements have exploded in the last few years, exponentially increasing the burden on business leaders to comply with governance, compliance and security demands. It is essential to manage regulatory risk and protect the business from data breaches and reputational damage. Data breaches also present the risk of catastrophic financial loss due to fines and penalties, some of which could be multiples of revenue.

Protection against breaches: The cornerstone of data value preservation

A data breach is one of the quickest ways to lose the entire value of your data asset investments, so physical and logical security must be at the forefront of your data platform strategy. Security measures include:

- Implementing robust technical measures and managing the risks associated with people accessing the platform

- Introducing controls to ensure that data platforms comply with relevant laws and regulations, enabling secure storage and access to data

- Ensuring data is being processed ethically, with the appropriate data privacy approach, so you control who has access to your private data

Control by design

Implementing control by design is the optimal way to ensure the appropriate controls are in place. Rather than considering controls as an afterthought, they need to be built into your business-as-usual processes so they are implemented automatically. Many modern data platforms now cater for control by design, taking care of governance, compliance and security. While these platforms will not entirely remove the burden, they will lighten the load, especially in preventing data breaches.

Cloud data platform hosting location

Choosing the appropriate hosting location for your data platform is crucial for maintaining compliance and security. When selecting a hosting location, it is essential to consider several key factors:

- **Jurisdiction.** The jurisdiction in which your data is stored and processed can significantly impact your requirements for compliance with data protection regulations. Countries have different laws that must be adhered to.

- **Data sovereignty.** Specific industries or regulations may require that data remains within specific geographic boundaries.

- **Physical security.** Evaluating measures such as access controls, surveillance, and protection against environmental risks for your data centre is of paramount importance. The potential risks associated with the location should also be weighed up, including natural disasters or political instability. All risks need to be carefully assessed to ensure robust disaster-recovery and business-continuity plans.

- **Network latency, particularly for real-time applications and user experience.** The proximity of the data centre to your primary user base can impact the performance and responsiveness of your data platform, making it a crucial factor in the overall effectiveness of your deployment.

Primary control considerations

The primary considerations for control are as follows:

- **Data privacy and security.** Ensure compliance with regulations like GDPR (EU), CCPA (California) and POPIA (South Africa). This involves anonymising, masking, pseudonymising and securing data to prevent breaches through access control, encryption and regular audits.

- **Data ownership and access.** Your data platform needs to be able to assign and manage data ownership and control who has access to your data, ensuring that access is restricted to authorised individuals only, thereby reducing the risk of internal breaches.

- **Transparency and accountability.** Your platform should provide a complete lineage of data movement from source to target and maintain access logs, both of which are required for control audits.

Managing the human factor

The human element is the most vulnerable aspect of any security strategy, with comprehensive measures critical to addressing this factor. Regular employee awareness and training programmes are essential to educate staff about potential threats and to instil best practices for safeguarding data. Access controls must be robust, to ensure that employees have access only to the information necessary for their roles. These controls need to incorporate:

- Role-based access

- Multi-factor authentication

- Zero trust

- The principle of least privilege (PoLP)***

Other vital security measures include:

- **A comprehensive incident response plan.** This is vital for effectively addressing data breaches, malware attacks and other security incidents.

- **Background checks.** Conducting thorough background checks on employees who handle sensitive data further mitigates the risk of insider threats.

- **Monitoring and auditing.** Robust monitoring and auditing systems need to be in place to detect anomalies and suspicious activities, ensuring that potential security breaches are promptly identified and addressed.

*** The principle of least privilege: Also known as the principle of minimal privilege (PoMP) or the principle of least authority (PoLA), PoLP prescribes that each user or process has privileges to access only the data that is essential to their role. It is a fundamental security measure to protect against unauthorised access and other data breaches.

- **Data loss prevention (DLP) solutions.** These can help prevent unauthorised data transfers and leakage, adding an additional layer of security to protect sensitive information.

Additional security measures

Beyond human factors, several technical and procedural measures are critical to ensuring the security of a data platform. These include:

- **Encryption.** It is fundamental that data is encrypted at rest and in transit to protect it from unauthorised access.

- **Network security.** Firewalls, secure network configurations, and intrusion detection and prevention systems will safeguard against external threats.

- **Vulnerability management.** Regular assessments and timely patching of systems and applications are essential in addressing security weaknesses. Maintaining regular backups of critical data and rigorously testing the recovery process ensures that data can be restored in the event of a loss.

- **Business continuity and disaster recovery (BCDR) plans.** Developing and testing comprehensive BCDR plans is essential to minimise downtime and data loss during unexpected events.

- **Third-party vendor management.** Evaluate the security practices of third-party vendors and service providers as part of a broader third-party risk management strategy.

Adopting a recognised security framework such as ISO 27001 or the NIST Cybersecurity Framework can provide a structured approach to implementing these security measures and help ensure that all aspects of the data platform are adequately protected.

If you suspect compliance, security, data ethics, privacy or access control shortcomings, consider starting with relevant audits to identify gaps and then execute the projects to address the deficiencies raised. The stakes are high today, with fines, penalties, reputational damage and potential personal incarceration all driving the requirement to be on top of your game. Overlooking governance could lead to a senseless security oversight that could jeopardise the value and reputation you have worked hard to build.

4. Collaboration: Driving value by building partnerships

If you skipped the section above – 'Control: Platform governance, compliance and security' – go back and read it. Closing your eyes and hoping someone else has that under control could have catastrophic consequences.

The data platform must enable secure, efficient sharing of data and insights – within the company and externally – driving cost savings and efficiency. Modern data platforms enable partnerships and collaboration on shared datasets. Platforms with built-in collaboration features enhance communication, knowledge sharing and value delivery in data analytics.

Internal collaboration

Data analytics teams often prefer to manage their own infrastructure, retaining control and circumventing IT involvement, but this can lead to duplication of processes and governance challenges. It is better to establish a collaboration mechanism with IT to enable the control and efficiency required by the data analytics function.

This presents a vital optimisation opportunity, enabling you to leverage existing IT governance, risk and compliance processes to manage your data platform. You can also reuse your existing IT helpdesk processes for data-related support requests. You might need to arm-wrestle your CIO to get their agreement on this, though.

External collaboration

It is ideal to cultivate a partnership mindset with vendors to maximise your benefit from these relationships. Building strong partnerships unlocks opportunities for innovation and growth that you might otherwise struggle to achieve. Vendors may also offer discounts, professional services and training allowances for long-term commitments or customer references.

Actively seek and leverage internal and external collaboration opportunities to accelerate value delivery and reduce data platform costs. Remember, collaboration is a powerful catalyst for reaching new heights in your data analytics journey.

5. Reliability: The backbone of critical business operations

Data platform reliability is essential for maintaining stakeholder confidence. A stable platform supports uninterrupted business operations and ensures the reliability of insights, thereby strengthening trust.

Legacy technologies may struggle with increased data volumes and new diverse data formats, leading to reliability issues. Upgrading to modern technologies can immediately enhance stability and reliability.

To minimise downtime and ensure rapid recovery, establish incident response processes and an active support desk. Proactive maintenance and active monitoring and alerts will help resolve issues before they impact business operations.

Ensuring the reliability of insights delivered by your data platform is three-fold:

1. Your platform must be stable

2. Your approach to delivering insights must be rock solid (refer to Chapter Six)

3. You must instil trust in your data analytics results (refer to Chapter Eight)

Reliability is crucial for incorporating valuable insights into critical business operations. Without confidence in your platform's reliability, investment will slow, limiting growth and shifting focus to cost management. Business leaders will also not rely on an unreliable platform to drive impactful decisions.

Investing in a highly reliable platform unlocks new opportunities to generate value by integrating analytics into business processes. Building confidence will encourage alignment, investment and accelerated value delivery.

6. Optimisation: Ensuring high performance and continuous improvement

Slow data platforms disrupt decision-making and efficiency and can lead to silos and shadow capabilities. Business leaders tend to prioritise progress over perfection and have limited tolerance for underperformance. They will quickly set up alternatives or outsource their data platform requirements.

Constant maintenance is needed to keep data platforms at peak performance levels. A sluggish platform loses value and increases risk, cost and complexity. Platforms are complex, which means performance degradation is expected.

However, slow performance does not necessarily mean a new platform is needed. This section explores ways to improve performance without upgrading.

Leveraging detailed monitoring for performance improvement

Detailed monitoring is your primary tool to improve platform performance. Monitoring each process, comparing it against benchmarks, and summarising weaknesses helps identify bottlenecks and allocate resources effectively. This transparency boosts the accountability of your technical teams, which can lead to immediate performance improvements. Skeletons in your data platform closet should not be tolerated.

Addressing skill gaps for optimal platform performance

Challenges often arise when migrating to a new platform with the same team, as they may try to operate it like the old one, or they may need more expertise.

Data engineers may hesitate to ask for help, making identifying skill gaps through assessments or other means essential. Assessing and training key team members may be necessary to maintain peak platform performance. Refer to Chapter Five for more on team management.

Optimisation in consumption-based cloud platforms

In consumption-based cloud platforms, optimisation directly impacts cost management. A sluggish platform can lead to higher compute costs due to inefficiencies. Ensure your team is certified on the platform, which will better equip them to optimise performance and reduce costs. They may benefit from shadowing an experienced consultant to build confidence in the platform.

Adopting a methodological approach to development

A methodological approach to development on any data platform will reduce the skill level required for optimal performance. A methodology that includes optimisation by design and automation improves performance and reduces costs, with build costs often dropping by more than 70% versus manual build costs.

7. Suitability: Fit-for-purpose data platform

Data and IT leaders sometimes struggle to justify data platform investments, claiming the value is unquantifiable but that the platform is necessary for future readiness. This can understandably lead to the questions:

- Future readiness for what?

- If value cannot be forecasted, why proceed with investing?

Data platform investments must align with the initiatives you plan to deliver to prevent you paying for unused platform components and features. Refer to Chapter Three if your team faces challenges with forecasting value.

Rationalising your data platform and capabilities

The first step in assessing suitability is to ensure your data platform has the necessary capabilities for your company's strategic objectives. Using the roadmap developed in Chapter Four, identify gaps by mapping your value-generating and foundational initiatives to your data platform capabilities. Your data analytics leader needs to maintain this capability matrix to streamline the planning process.

Next assess whether your team can effectively leverage the data platform to meet strategic objectives. Map your team's skills to the requirements of key initiatives and the platform's functionality. A skills audit may be necessary. Consider requiring vendor certification to enhance capabilities. Your data analytics leader should maintain a skills inventory for quick reference.

Combining the above considerations enables you to determine if your platform and team have the necessary capabilities for your data analytics roadmap. This analysis will also reveal whether you are effectively using all platform capabilities or whether you are paying for tools, components or features that are gathering digital dust.

This rationalisation helps streamline operations by identifying unused and overlapping tools, potentially leading to substantial cost savings, especially for larger companies. Simplifying your environment can reduce the total cost of ownership and improve efficiencies in platform maintenance and value delivery.

Avoid adopting unnecessary tools

To avoid unnecessary tool adoption, establish a phased approach that requires developing a minimum viable product (MVP) before considering new tools. The MVP approach will help validate whether a solution works and ensure processes are established before you adopt new technology.

Establishing processes before selecting technology platforms allows for intentional choices instead of you falling prey to the persuasions of salespeople.

Vendors may push features you don't need, but a clear process helps avoid unnecessary purchases driven by FOMO.

A phased approach to technology implementation can save millions in wasted investments and will speed up implementation by avoiding prolonged, failed attempts to find suitable tools.

Ensuring your data platform is fit for purpose will help manage costs, reduce complexity and accelerate the delivery of valuable insights.

Common pitfalls and how to avoid them

A data platform journey is filled with pitfalls. Avoid investing in new technology solely to follow trends, mitigate perceived risks, compete with rivals or satisfy stakeholders. Invest only if you can directly link the decision to a value driver and actively manage that value.

Do not underestimate the costs of data platform implementation or migration. Beyond platform costs, expect significant integration and people costs. As a client of ours put it, adding *integration* to any project doubles the budget, while *seamless integration* requires ten times the budget.

Final thoughts: Building a value-optimised data platform

As we conclude this chapter, think of your data platform as the foundation of a skyscraper. Just as a solid foundation ensures that a towering building remains stable, your data platform must be robust, adaptable and strategically aligned to support the weight of your company's objectives.

This chapter has equipped you with the critical elements to transform your data platform from a technical necessity into a strategic enabler of business growth. Remember, every step you take towards optimising your platform is a step towards realising your company's full potential. You are not just managing technology but building a legacy of innovation and growth. By focusing on adaptability, meticulous cost management and robust security, you now have the tools to overcome value constraints. Like a skyscraper, your platform must withstand the storms of business demands, while also ensuring the integrity of the insights it delivers.

Remember, though, that a skyscraper's foundation is just the beginning. The true strength lies in how your data platform supports the value your business builds over time. The AC³ROS framework is the bedrock on which your future data analytics-led initiatives will stand. Using the framework is not about creating something impressive for today. It is about constructing a platform that sustains your company's growth, innovation and resilience for years to come.

While futureproof platforms may not exist, future-proof frameworks do. With the AC³ROS framework, your data platform can adapt as your company's needs evolve, ensuring continued value realisation.

As we move into the next chapter for the final part of the RAPPID Value Cycle, we will focus on data trust – ensuring that the insights your data platform delivers are reliable. Without data trust, even the most advanced platform is like a skyscraper with faulty wiring – one short circuit away from disaster.

Key chapter takeaways

- Focus on value realisation over flashy features when making data platform investments. Ensure that every upgrade or change is directly tied to measurable business outcomes.

- Adaptability is crucial. Your data platform must scale with evolving business needs while maintaining a healthy ROI, ensuring you can meet future demands without costly overhauls.

- A value-based mindset must drive cost management. Utilise cost analysis tools to align expenses with the value generated and avoid unnecessary investments or migrations.

- Strong governance, compliance and security practices are non-negotiable. Prioritise these to protect your data assets and avoid costly breaches that can undermine your platform's value or, worse, harm your company.

- Internal and external collaboration are key to maximising the value of your data platform. Leverage partnerships to enhance efficiency, innovation and growth.

- Your data platform's reliability underpins its effectiveness. Invest in stable, modern technologies and proactive maintenance to ensure uninterrupted business operations.

- Optimisation is an ongoing process. Regularly monitor and refine your platform's performance to prevent inefficiencies that could lead to higher costs and reduced value delivery.

- Ensure your data platform is fit for purpose. Align its capabilities with your strategic objectives to avoid paying for unused features, and to streamline operations for better efficiency and cost-effectiveness.

A NOTE FOR DIVISIONAL AND SUBSIDIARY LEADERS

As you navigate the complexities of managing a data platform within a division or subsidiary, you must recognise the unique challenges you face. Budget constraints and limited autonomy in platform selection often require you to work within predefined systems and strict financial constraints. These factors can make it difficult to fully implement the adaptability and scalability discussed in this chapter. Additionally, your reliance on shared corporate services might slow down critical optimisations and integrations, impacting your ability to align divisional needs with broader corporate data analytics-led initiatives.

There are still opportunities to improve efficiency within your limitations. Focus on building strong collaborations across functions and divisions to drive efficiency and value creation. Ensure that your data governance practices are robust and aligned with corporate standards, while also addressing the specific needs of your division.

By strategically navigating these challenges, you can effectively leverage your data platform to support your division's growth and contribute to the overall success of your division and the greater group.

EIGHT

Data Trust – The BREATH Framework

D ata trust is pivotal to the success of data analytics-led initiatives. Without it, even the most sophisticated analytics can lead to misguided decisions, eroding confidence in your insights and jeopardising business outcomes. With the right approach, building data trust can become a crucial driver of success for your company, enabling confident decision-making and ensuring sustained value from your data analytics-led initiatives.

This chapter explores the BREATH framework, a comprehensive approach to building and sustaining data trust in your company. You will discover how to establish transparency, enforce accountability and maintain data health, all while navigating the challenges of scaling data analytics across complex environments.

Using examples, we will illustrate common pitfalls and provide actionable strategies to help you build the trust needed to make data analytics-driven decisions confidently.

The trust deficit: The hidden cost of mismatched data

The following example illustrates the real-world challenges many companies encounter with data analytics, highlighting the essential role of trust in driving value. Unlike oversimplified marketing hype, this example serves as a stark reminder that achieving success with data analytics is a complex and demanding journey. There are no shortcuts. As a business leader, you may recognise the familiar elements in this scenario, as companies above a certain size and complexity frequently grapple with these very issues.

EXAMPLE: Confusion at The Cleaning House

You are the chief marketing officer and an executive committee (ExCo) member of The Cleaning House, a leading seller of cleaning products. Your company's board has issued a directive to investigate declining revenues from your main product lines. Product X – your flagship product and key revenue driver – has recently suffered a sharp decline in sales and profit margins. This is critical, as Product X, until recently, contributed up to 15% of company revenues.

The CEO calls an emergency ExCo meeting, stating 'Everything else is on hold until we determine our recovery plan for Product X.'

At the meeting your market intelligence team kicks off by presenting recent trends and competitor analysis. Nothing particularly insightful comes out of the analysis – the market seems stable, and your competitors are not doing anything extraordinary (that you know of). The team is eager to delve into deeper analysis to uncover what is going wrong with Product X.

The company's top data scientist presents trend lines and forecasts, but there is an immediate snag. The reports use product codes – SKUs (stock-keeping units) – instead of product names, leading to confusion. Even for Product X, your bestseller, multiple packaging formats (single units, boxes, pallets) mean multiple SKUs, complicating the analysis.

The room grows uneasy as confidence in the data wavers. The COO, through a quick call to one of his team members, retrieves the correct SKUs for Product X, and the data scientist updates the report filters to reflect those. Questions still linger about the correctness of the SKUs. An hour into the meeting, value-driving decisions remain elusive.

The CFO is particularly sceptical. Seeking reassurance, she asks the data scientist to show revenue and unit sales data from the past six months, matched to finance data. The data scientist's face pales as he explains that mismatches between the ordering and finance systems' SKUs remain unresolved.

This revelation leads to murmurs of frustration and a discussion about the severity of the issue, noting that it wasn't corrected after last year's ordering system upgrade. Eventually, the CIO, who was originally accountable for resolving the SKU mismatch, tries to shift focus. He states, 'We are here to determine the recovery plan for Product X, not discuss system issues.' The meeting collectively disagrees, recognising that the system issues are obstructing the analysis and hindering the development of a recovery plan for Product X.

The CFO, still uneasy but with the clock ticking well into the second hour, suggests a quick reconciliation with finance data to develop some comfort. The figures align somewhat, but doubts about the accuracy linger. Not wanting to get held up by unreconciled differences, the CFO moves the meeting forward. Time is running out, and decisions need to be made.

The analysis presented reveals that the decline in Product X's revenue, margin and unit sales began six weeks ago, coinciding with the start of the financial year. What triggered this on the first day of the new year?

The team discusses potential causes of the margin decline, initially suspecting raw material price increases. The CFO contests that prices are locked in by a three-year supplier agreement, shifting the debate to what else is included in product cost. Are only raw material costs included, or are fixed manufacturing costs included too? What about transport, handling and storage costs? Should the margin calculation be changed to be more relevant for this exercise? The debate continues and confusion grows, with the meeting now way off track.

Finally, the CEO refocuses the discussion on resolving the issues with Product X. With the meeting reaching its fourth hour, the CEO reminds the team that he only has one week to deliver a recovery plan to the board. He wonders to himself whether, at this rate, a month would suffice.

While clambering for a clue, the chief sales officer notices a mismatch between the SKUs for Product X on the report and the order forms. The code is also missing from the latest sales report. Could the SKU have changed at the beginning of the year? This discovery brings the team closer to the root cause, but the issue remains unresolved.

With this small but valuable insight, the team agrees that the next clue will likely come from knowing the exact source of the information on the report. However, they quickly discover that the data scientist pulled the data from the company's data lake, without clarity on its origins. The CIO mentions that a data catalogue created by his team might contain the missing data lineage information. On further inspection, though, the catalogue covers only privacy and security classifications, not the data's flow or integration.

The team cannot trace how the data lake was populated without clear documentation. The

CIO searches through old emails for relevant documentation but eventually gives up, realising that the documentation was last updated before the most recent changes.

Meanwhile, the CFO reviews policy documents in search of another clue. She eventually discovers an interesting but unknown detail – the product policy states that SKUs change when they are rebranded, when packaging is updated or when the manufacturing process changes. The meeting explodes with the realisation that there must have been a change to the SKUs, but the new codes were not updated across all systems and documents.

At this stage the CEO is going through all five stages of grief simultaneously. With energy levels low and patience wearing thin, and with the meeting now crossing the six-hour mark, doubts grow about how it will be possible to present a plan to the board within a week.

The CEO instructs the COO, CDAO and CIO to ensure this situation does not recur. However, you wonder whether anything will change, given that similar issues were raised before. You secretly hope that ExCo meetings will not continue to be bogged down by system and data problems – the company has more critical challenges.

To wrap up the meeting, the CEO makes several assumptions to form at least a rudimentary result of the analysis, reasoning that 'Some action is better than no action'. He directs the team to raise Product X's price to offset margin declines, despite warnings that this may reduce demand. The CEO also instructs you and the product team to explore new product lines to compensate for potential volume losses.

The meeting ends with a collective sigh of relief, but lingering doubts remain about the effectiveness of the action plan.

A few days later the CEO receives a customer complaint about being unable to find Product X on the price list or website. It quickly becomes clear that the new SKUs were updated internally, but customers were not informed. This oversight caused the sales decline. Further investigation reveals that reduced sales volumes led to missed purchasing targets, resulting in higher raw material costs and reduced margins.

The CEO is astonished that the whole leadership team spent an entire day without being able to uncover the root cause, only for a single customer email to reveal it all. The CEO takes a deep BREATH, feeling relieved but recognising the urgent need to instil trust in their data and insights.

Ditch the hunch. Embrace the crunch. Take a deep BREATH.

Companies that effectively leverage data for decision-making naturally outperform their peers. Just as the body needs oxygen, companies need data analytics and insights to function optimally.

Think of this as VO2 max for your business. VO2 max is a measurement of your fitness level based on your body's use of oxygen. A lack of data trust hampers your company's ability to act decisively when it matters most, just as an unfit person huffs and puffs when climbing a flight of stairs.

The BREATH framework will help you build the vital foundations for data trust. Like a good fitness programme, this will support your company's ability to drive value creation through data analytics. No more huffing and puffing your way through emergency ExCo meetings.

Data trust is the confidence to derive insights from accurate, reliable data; and to act on the results within the window of maximum value without requiring additional confirmation.

Trust is built not through a single action but through multiple factors working together. Just as you build fitness through exercise, the more you apply these trust factors, the better your company will become at generating value through data analytics. The factors fall into two main categories:

1. Trust in the ability to use data confidently, which deals with the ability to interpret data analytics results and derive insights

2. Trust in the data itself, which depends on the availability of important additional information that builds understanding in the data and validates insights

The following diagram highlights these two categories.

The converging components of data trust

The next diagram illustrates the various components of the BREATH framework for data trust, all of which need to be in alignment for trust in your data analytics results to be created.

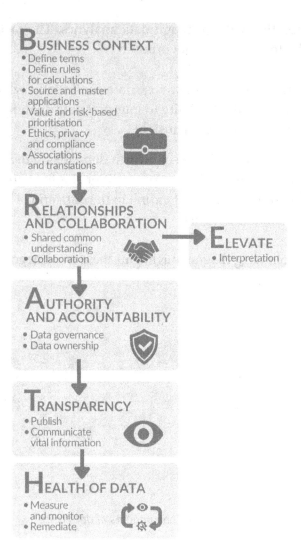

The BREATH framework for data trust

The BREATH framework for building and sustaining data trust

Using the earlier example of The Cleaning House, we will now explain the various dimensions of the BREATH framework in context. This approach will enable you to identify practical steps to build trust in your reporting and analytics, ensuring that your insights drive confident, value-generating action. BREATH stands for:

1. Business context

2. Relationships and collaboration

3. Elevate

4. Authority and accountability

5. Transparency

6. Health of data

1. Business context

Business context refers to the unique environment within which your company operates.

Every country has its laws, terminology and customs. It takes time to adapt to these different rules and languages, and as an outsider, you need to proceed cautiously to avoid unintentional mistakes. Similarly, companies have specific terminology, regulations and policies. Business context ensures everyone in the company shares a common language, facilitating better communication and understanding.

Building business context for your data is crucial for driving decisive actions from your insights. This involves:

- Clearly defining business-specific terms (especially contentious terms)

- Explicitly defining calculation rules

- Tracking data sources used for analytics

- Other key factors, explored below

Defining contentious terms

Clear business terminology is essential for building trust in data analytics. Without agreed definitions for key terms, uncertainty arises. Progress towards building data trust is stalled until these terms are defined.

The Cleaning House faced several challenges that could have been avoided with well-defined business terms. A notable issue was the confusion over the term *product cost*. The team debated whether it included only raw material costs or other factors as well. Had there been a clear, approved definition for product cost, the meeting could have quickly resolved the issue, saving time and maintaining trust. The cost of low data trust is a lack of clarity that leads to uncertainty and delayed decision-making.

Business terms need to be documented formally in a business glossary and made accessible for consumption. They are especially valuable when published alongside analytics results in relevant reports and dashboards. This context enhances the clarity of insights and boosts confidence in decision-making.

Explicitly define rules used for calculations

To extract valuable insights from reports and dashboards, rules and calculations applied to the data must be explicitly defined. These should extend logically from the definition of business terms.

In The Cleaning House meeting, when battling with their understanding of product cost while analysing margins, trust would have been reinforced if the data scientist had been able to verify that the calculation used in the report aligned with an established and approved definition of product cost.

Documented calculations that align with business terms are vital for building trust, especially with complex concepts. This underscores the need for precise term definitions, as accurate calculations hinge on correctly defined and approved terms. Rules can also apply specific criteria to data, such as showing only active products or excluding certain customer segments to enable a more focused view.

Like business terms, documented rules and calculations need to be accessible alongside reports and dashboards. Imagine how much trust would have been built in The Cleaning House meeting if the terms and calculations for the report were available on the report itself.

Ideally, analytics should include these definitions to answer questions instantly, reducing the need for further investigation, and speeding up decision-making. This confidence will encourage more frequent use of data analytics, improving value creation and instilling a culture of data-informed decisions.

Source application and master application

Users often have preconceived notions about the lack of reliability of data from different business applications and data sources. If there is a known data issue with your CRM system but users know your recently implemented billing system has clean data, they will naturally have more trust in reports from the billing system.

Classifying your business applications and data sources is essential to identify a master application for each data area (e.g., customer, product, billing). The master application is the definitive source for specific data elements, and all other applications and analytics tools must pull from that as the most up-to-date and reliable source.

Doubts were raised when The Cleaning House's executives questioned the source of the data. Explicitly referencing the data's origin on the dashboard would have immediately increased trust, especially if that source was a classified master application.

Trust is reinforced when the source of data and any calculations, groupings, or filters applied are documented. Users need to know whether they are seeing *raw data* or *altered data*, and if altered, which calculations have been applied or how the data has been changed.

Therefore, publishing the data lineage – source applications, master application classifications and applied calculations – on the report or dashboard is a valuable practice for building data trust.

Value and risk-based prioritisation

Not all datasets are equal in value or risk. Given the vast amounts of data companies generate, managing all data with the same level of care is unfeasible. To optimise your focus, develop a metric that scores datasets based on their value to the business and the associated risks. Prioritise managing data that drives critical insights, decisions and key business processes, while considering the risk of neglecting certain datasets.

Value-based prioritisation ensures you concentrate your resources on the data that generates the most value. However, risk must also be factored into your approach. If mismanaged or ignored, some low-value datasets might carry significant risks such as compliance violations or operational disruptions. Conversely, high-value datasets might also have high risks that need careful management to avoid negative consequences.

In The Cleaning House meeting, understanding the value and risk of specific datasets would have helped leaders prioritise efforts more effectively, focusing resources on areas where the positive or negative impact would be most significant. This dual consideration would have enabled a more balanced and strategic approach to managing the company's data, generating improved results.

Ethics, privacy and compliance

Using data for decision-making is complex when policies govern the ethical use of private information. If users have confidence, they will gain trust in using the data correctly. Including ethics, privacy and compliance guidelines in reports, alongside relevant data, will build trust by clarifying what users can do with the data and which policies govern its use. Compliance guidelines must cover the broad range of your regulatory landscape, including corporate policies and specific agreements related to, for example, mergers and acquisitions. They must also consider any region-specific regulations for multinationals.

Beyond your ethics, privacy and compliance requirements being published, they must be enforced on a technical level. This takes your company beyond perceived compliance to a place where risk is automatically managed and monitored, providing you with the confidence needed for your data analytics journey to reach its full potential.

Association and translation

Raw data often contains complex technical descriptions, and technical jargon needs to be translated for the business context. Imagine the data scientist showing charts with technical tags like *O_QTY* and *U_PCE*. While technical users are familiar with them, these tags are meaningless to most business users.

Trust in data is built by translating technical jargon into everyday business language, often through a business data model or semantic layer. Seeing *Order quantity* instead of O_QTY and *Unit price* instead of U_PCE will make data more accessible. This translation bridges the gap between technical data and business context, enhancing trust and making the data more useful for decision-making.

2. Relationships and collaboration

Trust in data analytics is built by actively managing relationships between data and people. Collaboration around data is essential for building trust. This requires establishing a shared understanding of your data (see 'Business context' above) and fostering communication between data, IT and business stakeholders. This collaboration is the glue that holds everything together.

Relationships and collaboration can be enforced by implementing shared KPIs or OKRs across areas of concern (using value and risk-based prioritisation). The best relationships are where the value generated through collaboration is measurable and enforceable.

Shared common understanding

In The Cleaning House meeting, the CIO mentioned his team's data catalogue, which initially focused on privacy and security. However, a data catalogue is more than just a compliance tool – it is an asset that is valuable for sharing knowledge about the company's data.

Using a data catalogue to share knowledge improves trust by making data more accessible, leading to more reliable insights. The data catalogue stores most of the components of the BREATH framework (known as metadata), making the data catalogue a foundational element for building data trust – essentially a *data trust repository*.

Collaboration

The Cleaning House struggles with communication. Executives hold critical information but fail to share it actively. Think about the CIO's surprise reveal of the data catalogue. An emergency ExCo meeting is not the time for this important information to come to light. Establish processes and structures that encourage continuous collaboration and information sharing.

Effective communication, especially regarding changes, is essential. ExCo meetings might not be the best forum. Consider implementing the communication strategies discussed in the 'Data governance' section below – such as forums and clear escalation paths – to manage data-related communication effectively.

3. Elevate

Data analytics and insights are valuable only if consumers can understand and apply them effectively. Your company's leaders and analytics users must be equipped with the skills and confidence to interpret data, extract valuable insights and apply those insights effectively to drive value. This is one of the most notable differentiators between companies that drive substantial value through data analytics and those that do not. The one-percenters build their companies on data analytics, a core component of their strategy, and this agenda is driven directly by their C-suite leaders.

Interpretation: Trust in the ability to use the data

Just as email and spreadsheet skills became essential in the past, interpreting data, extracting valuable insights and applying those insights effectively to drive value are now critical skills for business leaders. Some companies have yet to learn the potential of data to drive value when it is applied correctly and is well understood. Leaders must develop these skills to drive value in a data-centric world. Without this ability, leaders may lack trust in the data, even if it is reliable, missing opportunities to apply the insights to generate value.

Business leaders may hesitate to admit difficulties in leveraging data analytics. Address these challenges in one-on-one settings to ensure leaders gain confidence in their abilities.

4. Authority and accountability

The Cleaning House operates in organised chaos when it comes to its data. No single point of accountability exists for specific datasets, and directives for resolving issues are unclear and untracked, leading to confusion and misinterpretation.

Trust in insights will remain low unless accountability is strengthened through clear data governance and ownership, assigned at the highest level. Leaders must increase their data-confidence and take responsibility for improving data quality.

Data governance

The Cleaning House needs a dedicated data governance structure, as there is no formal platform or forum to which critical data issues can be escalated. The lack of governance led to the derailment of the emergency ExCo meeting, where no informed decisions could be made due to limited data trust and clarity. Data issues identified in similar meetings should be delegated to a formal forum for resolution.

Establish a formal data governance structure, including a forum with defined responsibilities and escalation paths, chaired by a C-level sponsor, with each business area represented by a decision-maker. This ensures dedicated focus on data issues and direct accountability at a senior level. The data governance structure needs to focus on creating processes that build data trust, fostering continuous improvement. This will prevent operational issues from disrupting ExCo meetings.

Data ownership

At The Cleaning House, unclear data ownership leads to friction and siloed efforts to resolve issues. Data ownership must be centralised with a single point of accountability, ensuring all parties answer to a designated accountable leader.

Improve data ownership by identifying core data entities in the company – like finance, operations, marketing, customer, product, etc – and assigning a formal data owner to each data domain. These data owners are held accountable for managing the data health in their specific domain by executing the relevant initiatives sanctioned by the data governance structure.

Data owners are solely responsible for their assigned domains, making it clear who to approach for any issues related to specific data entities. When data ownership is formalised and well understood, decision-making can be accelerated.

5. Transparency

When supporting information to understand data is limited, data trust is eroded. Transparency involves publishing accurate information widely and sharing critical data-related updates across the company.

Publishing data trust metrics

The Cleaning House lacks the supporting information to build trust in its report's insights. Key data trust elements, all of which have been referred to in the previous sections of this chapter, should be published alongside analytics results to enhance trust. The following example of a data trust dashboard illustrates these components.

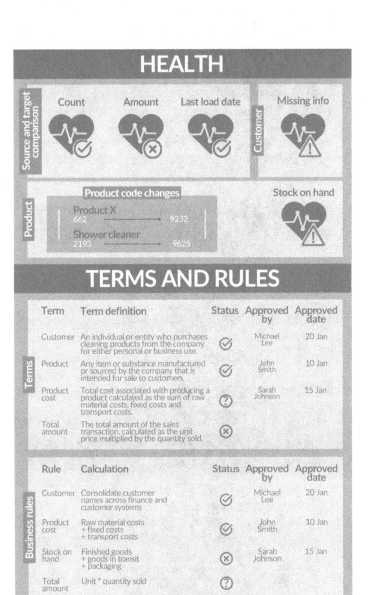

Example of a data trust dashboard (part 1)

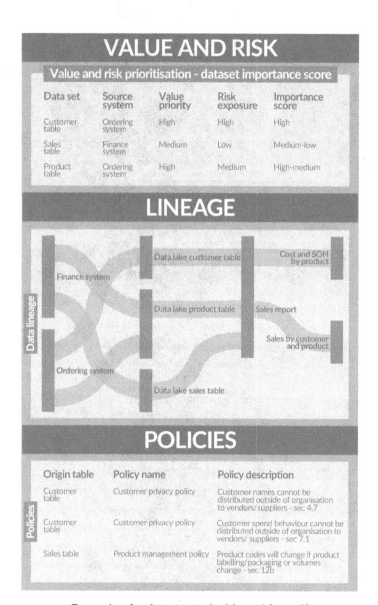

VALUE AND RISK

Value and risk prioritisation - dataset importance score

Data set	Source system	Value priority	Risk exposure	Importance score
Customer table	Ordering system	High	High	High
Sales table	Finance system	Medium	Low	Medium-low
Product table	Ordering system	High	Medium	High-medium

LINEAGE

Data lineage

Finance system

Ordering system

Data lake customer table

Data lake product table

Data lake sales table

Cost and SOH by product

Sales report

Sales by customer and product

POLICIES

Policies

Origin table	Policy name	Policy description
Customer table	Customer privacy policy	Customer names cannot be distributed outside of organisation to vendors/suppliers - sec 4.7
Customer table	Customer privacy policy	Customer spend behaviour cannot be distributed outside of organisation to vendors/suppliers - sec 7.1
Sales table	Product management policy	Product codes will change if product labelling/packaging or volumes change - sec 12b

Example of a data trust dashboard (part 2)

> If you want more information about our data trust dashboard, and for a downloadable version, visit this link:
> **rappidvaluecycle.com/datatrustdashboard**

Communicating critical data information

The Cleaning House could have managed its data more effectively when implementing the upgraded ordering system, which led to discrepancies with finance data. Essential information impacting business areas must be communicated early to enable remediating actions and prevent erosion of data trust. A data governance structure is a powerful information-sharing system to track initiatives required to manage the company's data effectively.

Effective communication ensures that all stakeholders affected by changes related to data, processes, context or applications are informed promptly – ideally before the next emergency ExCo meeting is called. Without the required structures, data issues tend to fall by the wayside, becoming a priority only when the data is required for a specific project or initiative and value realisation has already been delayed.

Value can be lost when information is withheld, regardless of the reason it is withheld. Instead of thinking, *What would happen if they had access to this information?,* think the converse: *What would happen if they did not have this information?* Transparency in sharing relevant information drives the effectiveness of your leaders in driving value for the company.

6. Health of data

Health of data focuses on data quality, measured against dimensions like accuracy, completeness and timeliness. It also involves remediating data quality issues to manage data proactively.

Measure and monitor

The Cleaning House needs to measure and monitor data quality. Comparing similar data across applications could reveal inconsistencies. Publishing these metrics alongside analytics fosters data trust.

For instance, a validation rule could have flagged the missing SKUs, saving hours of debate and allowing more time for decision-making. More importantly, the issue would have been picked up earlier, potentially saving millions in lost revenue.

Measuring data quality also ensures compliance with internal policies and external regulations, further enhancing data trust. For example, product codes can be checked against policy requirements.

Remediate

Remediation aims to correct bad data and establish controls to prevent future issues. At The Cleaning House, a policy change led to a damaging ripple effect when Product X's code was updated. Poor communication across business lines meant product codes were not updated in all systems, and customers stopped placing orders. This example shows how data management can directly impact revenue.

As a business leader, you need to recognise the risks associated with poor data management. Data governance structures must be empowered to establish formal remediation processes.

In this case, remediation could involve establishing an approval process for SKU changes, which enforces visibility for all affected parties. The data owner will be accountable for implementing this process and needs to ensure any changes are communicated across all relevant areas.

It is far more cost-effective to quickly identify and correct data issues before they enter business processes and applications. Once bad data is embedded, correction costs can escalate to an estimated hundredfold (based on the 1:10:100 rule mentioned in Chapter Five) versus the cost of preventative measures. Remediation must be planned and executed swiftly to avoid unnecessary expenses.

Final thoughts: Strengthening data trust for lasting success

Building trust in your data is like building the physical endurance of a marathon runner. Just as no athlete can reach their peak without a disciplined training regimen, no company can fully leverage its data without a structured approach to building trust. The BREATH framework provides the training plan to strengthen your company's trust in its data, enabling decisive action when it matters most.

Data trust is not a one-time achievement but an ongoing journey. It is a process that requires consistent effort across multiple dimensions:

- Understanding your business context

- Defining clear rules and terms

- Ensuring transparency

- Fostering collaboration and accountability through data governance

- Maintaining a focus on data health

By exploring the BREATH framework and understanding the actionable strategies within each component, you can build and sustain the data trust necessary to drive confident, value-generating decisions in your company.

As you move forward, challenge yourself and your team to take a proactive approach. You have already taken the first step by gaining an understanding of the BREATH framework. Now it is time to put your knowledge into action. Trust your ability to lead this transformation – success is within your reach. Start by establishing a formal data governance structure, creating a data catalogue – even a simple spreadsheet will work to begin with – and implementing a data trust dashboard. These steps will be your first on the path to building a company that operates confidently and with clarity.

With this chapter we have concluded our exploration of the RAPPID Value Cycle. We have covered recognising value, investing in insights, fostering a people and data value culture, establishing an approach for delivering insights, implementing your platform optimised for value, and building data trust. These components are essential to creating a robust, value-driven data analytics strategy.

In the next and final chapter we will introduce a pivotal role that will empower your company to aim for and assure value. This role is the final piece of the puzzle, ensuring that your data analytics-led initiatives deliver the tangible, measurable results your business demands. Let us take this final step together and unlock the full potential of your data analytics journey.

Key chapter takeaways

- Data trust is pivotal to the success of data analytics-led initiatives, ensuring that insights are accurate and reliable and lead to confident decision-making.

- Establishing clear business context, including defining contentious terms and calculation rules, is essential for building trust in data analytics.

- Transparency in data sources, data lineage and applied calculations is crucial for fostering trust among data users and ensuring the reliability of insights.

- Empowering business leaders with the skills and confidence to interpret and apply data insights effectively is key to driving value from data analytics.

- Effective data governance, including clear accountability and ownership of data domains, is necessary to maintain data health and prevent operational disruptions.

- Collaboration and communication between business, IT and data stakeholders are vital for building a shared understanding of data and driving value through data analytics.

- Regularly measuring and monitoring data quality, together with swift remediation of data issues, prevents costly errors and enhances trust in data analytics-driven decisions.

- Building data trust is an ongoing process that requires consistent effort across multiple dimensions, leading to sustained value from data analytics-led initiatives.

A NOTE FOR DIVISIONAL AND SUBSIDIARY LEADERS

Implementing the concepts from this chapter in your area of responsibility requires careful consideration of the unique challenges you face.

Ensuring alignment between your division's business context and that of the broader group is essential to maintain consistency in data interpretation and trust. Equally important is consistency in defining and applying rules across divisions. Variations can undermine trust and complicate data consolidation.

Establishing a formal data governance structure may be more complex in a multi-division environment, but it is crucial for cohesive data management. Transparency and open communication about data-related changes are vital in preventing confusion and fostering trust in your insights.

While the BREATH framework is designed to be flexible, you need to adapt its principles to fit your division's specific needs and constraints without compromising its effectiveness.

Finally, ensuring clear accountability for data quality and governance within your division, regardless of group mandates, will help maintain high standards and align with the broader group strategy. By addressing these challenges thoughtfully, you can build a strong foundation of data trust that empowers your division to produce data analytics-driven value effectively.

PART THREE
WHEN PRIORITIES COLLIDE: CALL ON THE MISSING LINK

NINE

Assuring Value From Strategic Data Analytics-Led Initiatives – The Data Value Assurance Framework

Throughout this book, we have debunked the myth that data analytics must aim to generate actionable insights. This myth is the largest contributor to the high failure rate of data analytics-led initiatives, with companies producing impressive but unembedded insights that yield little value, but require substantial investments to develop. As we have seen, success in data analytics is about more than generating actionable insights. It is about embedding those insights into business processes to drive real value.

Even in the most astute companies, this is a challenging feat due to the disparate priorities of C-level executives. It demands a strategic role that can move mountains in aligning cross-functional teams to shared objectives. In this chapter we introduce that mountain-moving role and the framework that is the foundation for its success, providing assurance of value from data analytics-led initiatives, a critical enabler of the RAPPID Value Cycle. This will build your data-confidence, enabling you to assertively invest in high-potential initiatives as you will be able to identify and mitigate the risks of failure.

We begin with a real-world example that illustrates a typical series of events that led to failure to realise any value from a high-potential initiative. You may be able to relate to this illustration.

CASE STUDY: How misalignment destroyed value creation

Years ago, we were consulted to help a large financial services company that faced a severe customer churn problem, with customers leaving faster than they were joining. The marketing team needed help pinpointing the reasons and asked us to build a customer churn analytics model as a last resort.

The project began, but we faced delays as IT initially denied access to the data we needed. Meanwhile, the business intelligence team provided only altered summaries that hid the nasty truths we were after. After multiple escalations and several weeks, during which customers continued to churn and the company continued to bleed revenue, we finally obtained the data we needed.

After months of testing, our model achieved 80% accuracy in predicting customers that would churn within the next ninety days. It took a massive effort from the team, who for months worked late into the night and on weekends to meet the deadline. Our valuable insights were profound and had the potential to save the company millions in lost revenue.

The next step in the project was to embed the results into the relevant business applications so that the retentions department could start taking targeted action to address the churn. Much to our surprise, though, we faced a wall of resistance.

We faced numerous questions in an inquisition-style meeting with the executives about the project's origin, funding and system changes required for implementation – areas outside our scope as data experts. It was as if our success in developing the model undermined their authority. The meeting descended into chaos, followed by a three-month delay to decide on the implementation strategy.

Eventually, we learned that five business application changes were necessary to integrate the churn model, requiring an external vendor and a six-month timeline. This news led to the project's cancellation, resulting in the resignation of two senior data team members and strained relationships across business functions. Much of the motivation to generate value and impact had been lost.

At that point, twelve months had passed since the project's initiation, and the business continued to decline due to customer churn.

Three years later, after restructuring, we were again asked to build a customer churn analytics model. External consultants identified a similar opportunity to protect revenue with a churn model. Have you ever paid consultants to tell you something you already knew?

Despite obtaining promises of support from IT for the now predictable application changes, the project was cancelled again for similar reasons, even though we had attempted to mitigate the risks.

Over the next few years, the company attempted the implementation several more times, spending around $20 million without success. Despite the failures, they continued to invest in the initiative, seemingly forgetting past lessons.

Early in our careers as data analytics leaders, we suffered a few similar failures. We painfully recall the experience of building valuable analytics models, only to run into walls of resistance when attempting to embed them into business processes to drive decisions and value. We often faced business leaders impressed by our successes, but they could not be convinced to adopt our models to drive their processes, no matter how hard we tried. Data platform reliability also sometimes played a role. We were stuck in a regressive spiral of value drain.

As we gained experience, we began playing the mountain-moving, strategic leadership role that we will introduce you to shortly. We had little choice – we desperately needed to see the value generated from our data analytics models. But there was no role that had any mandate for or interest in this value realisation, in the companies we were engaged with.

While we lacked a structured approach and were operating with a limited mandate, often as external consultants, the process was always cumbersome and challenging, and the outcomes, though valuable, were often suboptimal. In this chapter we will introduce you to the powerful framework we developed that increased our success rates within a shorter timeframe. This framework will also tremendously accelerate your ability to realise value through data analytics. But first we will explore the misalignment and dichotomy faced by CDAOs when trying to generate value through data analytics.

Overcoming conflicting priorities in data analytics-led initiatives

In data analytics-led initiatives, aligning priorities across different C-level executives can be a major challenge. An understanding of why this misalignment exists in the first place is essential in solving this challenge.

The evolution of IT leadership roles

Each C-level executive has distinct focus areas with minimal overlap. The CMO focuses on marketing, the CHRO on people, etc.

IT departments previously struggled to align their priorities with the needs of business stakeholders. They had challenges understanding whether their priority was to manage technology, to innovate, or to act as consultants that identify opportunities for optimisation. To address this confusion, a new role was created: the chief information officer (CIO). Everything technology-related now had a home in the company.

Realising a critical risk, the CIO had to bridge the gap between the company's technology and its objectives. Enterprise architects were introduced – experts who could act as translators between the two worlds. They ruled the roost in the IT world for many years.

Enterprise architects became pivotal in ensuring technology met company objectives, particularly during major organisation changes. The CIO drives IT strategy to align with the business strategy, while the enterprise architect ensures that the IT landscape is aligned with the IT and business strategies. Over time the enterprise architect role was formalised, with the TOGAF certification now serving as the benchmark for this discipline.[44]

The rise of the chief data and analytics officer (CDAO)

Data analytics, then called *business intelligence*, was initially managed by the CFO and the CIO. As time passed, companies began using data analytics as a strategic value driver, and the CFO–CIO combination could no longer manage the growing complexity.

Similar to how IT departments initially battled with their priorities, the role of this new data function was unclear. Was it to extract data, build reports and dashboards, or implement innovative solutions? Or was it meant to consult to the business on broader data management issues? To address this confusion, companies created the chief data officer (CDO) role, which evolved into the role of chief data and analytics officer (CDAO). Everything data-related now had a home in the company.

The CDO/CDAO priorities and areas of focus have been clarified through frameworks such as the *Cubic Framework for the Chief Data Officer*, helping this role progress along its evolving journey.[45]

Much like the CIO's alignment challenges, the CDAO also faces challenges in aligning data-related efforts with business priorities. However, fixing this is not as easy as appointing the data equivalent of an enterprise architect, because there is a third component that must also be aligned: IT.

It is important to understand that the CDAO, while working alone, can create only limited value. Real value emerges only when insights are integrated into business processes to drive better decisions across a broader range of employees. However, this requires changes to business processes owned by business functions, and integrations with business applications owned and managed by IT. Lacking control over a large portion of the value chain, or value cycle, data analytics functions shy away from these challenging integration requirements, instead choosing the comfort of producing actionable insights by building models, reports and dashboards. This vastly limits their potential to generate value.

The CDAO's challenge: Managing multiple priorities

No C-level executive has a direct *value* KPI. Value is contextualised differently across roles. For example, the CFO focuses on cash flow, the CHRO on staff retention, and the CIO on system uptime. Value is distributed across the company in disparate and often disconnected KPIs. When the CDAO arrives on the scene with a shiny new way to generate value, called data analytics, the company is often unprepared. Leadership focus remains on existing, disparate priorities that drive value in their respective areas, with their focus often reinforced by promises of personal reward.

The CIO also faces alignment challenges, but these are different. Often, IT selects and implements a technology such as a CRM system, and the business operates within the limits of the application's functionality. Although not ideal, IT often selects the technology first and then builds a business case around it.

This approach does not work for the CDAO, as business needs are presented first, without sufficient clarity. The CDAO must work with the business to find the best solution, while business leaders may not be clear yet about the decisions they want to drive from the insights, or how to embed the insights into existing processes and applications.

Compounding this complexity, different leaders in the same business function have varying data needs, driven by varying KPIs. The operations manager might be focused on detailed customer fault data, while the COO requires a summarised view of mean time to resolution by product and customer segment. They expect custom views and insights, and these must integrate with data across other business areas, as well as with business processes and IT-owned business applications.

When the CDAO pushes to integrate insights into processes for better decision-making, they often face resistance from business leaders, who can be very tentative when adopting new data analytics-driven approaches. They prefer to receive insights and decide for themselves how to use them, slowing progress.

Successful data analytics functions often rely on informal methods – such as their strong relationships with business and IT leaders – to embed their work into business processes and IT-managed applications. However, this approach is not always practical, especially for new data analytics functions without established reputations. As a result, cross-departmental limitations stifle innovation and dilute the potential of data analytics-driven value, compounding a regressive spiral of value drain.

To summarise this dichotomy: value from data analytics-led initiatives can only truly be realised when insights are integrated into business processes, driving value-generating, decisive actions across a broad range of users. However, many companies have yet to fully adapt to data analytics as a value-adding discipline. Both business and IT must be prepared to align to incorporate data analytics-driven decision-making. The gap is not technical, but one of alignment for value realisation, and most companies are far from achieving this, with no enterprise architect-equivalent role or TOGAF-equivalent certification on the horizon to rescue you ... until now.

Successful collaboration drives value in complex initiatives

The importance of cross-divisional collaboration for the success of complex initiatives cannot be overstated. Successful companies like Boeing, Apple, Ford, Toyota and John Deere have all demonstrated that integrating diverse business functions into a unified strategy is the key to successfully delivering complex initiatives. These cases, which we expand on below, highlight that complex initiatives succeed when key leaders drive alignment and collaboration across divisions.

Boeing's 787 Dreamliner project shows how close cooperation between international engineering and supply chain teams and third-party suppliers was essential to managing the intricacies of global manufacturing.[46] As discussed in Chapter Six, Apple's product development process, driven by Tim Cook, is another example of the tight integration of design, engineering and operations, which resulted in innovative products that transformed industries.

Similarly, Ford's One Ford strategy – under Alan Mulally's leadership – brought together teams from across the company to execute multiple complex initiatives, leading to a successful turnaround during a challenging economic period. Author and former Global 100 executive Sarah Miller Caldicott wrote about Mulally's impact, stating that prior to his tenure, executives leveraged vulnerabilities among their peers and prioritised self-preservation over collaboration. Mulally changed that. Executive meetings became an environment of collaboration and safety, where data could be shared without blame. This set the stage for innovation success.[47]

In Toyota's journey under Zack Hicks, the importance of cross-functional collaboration was paramount to driving value in complex initiatives. Hicks emphasised the integration of IT, data and business functions, highlighting the need for a unified approach where all new digital and traditional aspects are connected. By fostering agile, cross-skilled teams that worked closely with business stakeholders, Hicks ensured that Toyota's digital transformation efforts were aligned with business objectives, enabling rapid delivery of innovative solutions and maximising value for the company.[48]

Finally, under the leadership of Samuel Allen, who had a background in industrial management and engineering, John Deere successfully navigated the complexities of becoming more driven to generate value through data analytics.[49] Allen's strategic approach underscored the need for strong leadership that could unite various functions around a common objective – leveraging data to create value for customers. This collaborative effort brought together IT, data science and business operations to implement advanced technologies like IoT and data analytics within John Deere's Farm Forward vision, yielding outstanding results for the company.[50]

The lessons from these examples apply directly to your own data analytics-led initiatives, where collaboration between IT, business, and data analytics functions is crucial for establishing a positive value cycle for realising value. Ensuring all stakeholders are aligned and working towards the same goal is fundamental to success.

The missing link: A strategic, mountain-moving role

If generating value is your priority, complexity will be your friend. To manage this complexity and assure value from data analytics-led initiatives, you must eliminate silos by removing obstacles, bridging the gaps between data, IT and business. This chapter will formally introduce the role that will move these mountains for you. This is the role that, until now, has been missing from the data analytics value chain, or value cycle. This role is the *data value architect,* and it is enabled by the Data Value Assurance framework, which is explained later in this chapter.

Important considerations for the success of the data value architect (DVA) role include:

- **Purpose.** The purpose of the DVA is to realise value by achieving business objectives supported by data analytics-led initiatives. This role acts like the supply chain manager of the data analytics value chain.

- **Focus.** The DVA's focus is singular: generating value. While they may rely on project managers to support the delivery of specific initiatives, the DVA operates at a senior level and has the authority and responsibility to engage across the C-suite at the level of directors, vice presidents or equivalent, or at most one level below those roles.

- **Position for alignment.** The DVA is positioned at the intersection of data, IT and business priorities. When a business objective that can be supported by data analytics is identified, the DVA aligns the data analytics function with IT and business functions to ensure value realisation. When IT drives innovation, the DVA aligns that innovation with data analytics to enhance innovation and support business functions in generating value. Conversely, when data analytics drives innovation, the DVA aligns IT and business functions to ensure value is generated.

- **Position for impact.** The DVA must be positioned at a senior leadership level to bridge any gaps caused by varying priorities. The role is different from that of a traditional project manager, whose primary accountability lies in delivering projects on time and within budget, and assigning resources effectively. As the DVA bridges the gaps between data, IT and business, it should not reside within the data analytics function. We recommend the role reports to the CFO or the most influential C-level executive, ensuring they have the necessary context and mandate. Position the DVA to avoid internal politics, and provide them with full support to ensure they can generate value.

- **Responsibility.** The role title may vary, and you might assign the mandate to an existing leader. However, the accountability and responsibility of the DVA in realising and accelerating value are crucial.

We recommend that your data, IT and business teams wear steel-tip shoes to work because, with your DVA given the support to squeeze out every drop of value from your data, some toes will get stepped on.

Identifying a suitable candidate for the DVA role

The ideal candidate for the DVA role has strategic vision, technical expertise and strong interpersonal skills. They need experience in data analytics, IT and business operations, and a proven track record of successfully aligning cross-functional teams to achieve measurable value. Find someone who can navigate corporate politics, influence without direct authority, manage complex projects across multiple departments, and is willing to be guided by the Data Value Assurance framework.

As you consider implementing this role in your company, remember that you are laying the groundwork for substantial value creation. This role can potentially transform how your company leverages data analytics for success.

Why the CDAO should not take on the DVA role

At a recent air show we attended, thousands of visitors were trying to leave the parking lot simultaneously, causing gridlock at the end of a long day. For some reason, our queue moved faster than the others, creating frustration in other queues. We had a traffic officer at the intersection up ahead that favoured our queue. We wondered why, but as we got closer, he removed his reflector vest, jumped into a car in our queue, and drove off with his mates, having a good laugh. This chancer had prioritised our queue for his own benefit, leaving drivers in the other queues seething!

If you send the CDAO to do the DVA's job, there is a risk that they may prioritise their own 'queue', frustrating other stakeholders and undermining alignment efforts. An independent person directing the traffic can ensure balanced solutions that address all concerns and manage every risk.

The CDAO is already occupied with delivering data analytics-led initiatives. Asking them to also convince fellow executives to alter their priorities will likely divert their attention too far from their primary objectives.

The Data Value Assurance framework

A framework must guide the DVA to enable them to deliver value. The Data Value Assurance framework outlines the critical components for the DVA's success. In larger companies, this function may be carried out by a team, with various specialists executing the different components of the framework.

Later in this chapter we will also discuss considerations for forming a data value assurance team. By the end, you will have the context and justification to confidently invest in a DVA, whether as an individual or team. The appropriate scale depends on your company's size and value creation potential, which can be determined by applying the frameworks in Chapters Three and Four.

The Data Value Assurance framework ensures alignment across your company's functions, assuring value from data analytics-led initiatives. Companies often have complex structures and multiple accountability levels, making alignment difficult. Consider where your marketing, data analytics, operations and IT functions relate to one another. Are they aligned to, for example, seamlessly implement a customer churn analytics model, or is there potential for misalignment in priorities?

The DVA synchronises these areas, ensuring unity in priorities, alignment of objectives, and transparent communication, thus assuring efficient value realisation.

To achieve this, the Data Value Assurance framework has three main components:

1. Support

2. Contract

3. Deliver

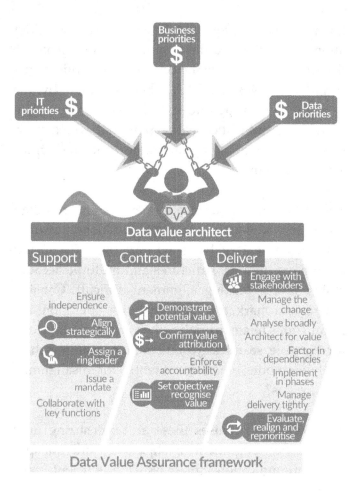

The collaborative role of the data value architect, based on the
Data Value Assurance framework

1. Support: Enabling the DVA's success

The success of your DVA hinges on support from executive leadership. They will face resistance – priority shifts, changes in performance metrics, and process alterations – often with limited resources and influence. To enable them, ensure the following support measures are in place:

Ensure independence

The DVA should be positioned independently to avoid bias. This role is best placed with the executive that has value creation as a primary focus, which will look different from company to company. Finance could be a suitable placement to ensure independence. Alternatively, consider the chief strategy office or another neutral environment to keep the focus on value and minimise their involvement in corporate politics.

Align strategically

The DVA's initiatives need to be linked directly to strategic objectives to keep them at the forefront of the company's strategic focus. You will already have a good idea of these objectives from work done in Chapter Three to identify value.

Assign a ringleader

A senior decision-maker should be assigned to support the DVA. This ringleader needs direct ties to the highest authority and influence across business functions. They must take accountability for supporting the DVA's efforts. This can be the ringleader assigned in Chapter Four.

Issue a mandate

The ringleader or CEO needs to issue a clear directive to stakeholders with authority over the various business functions involved in implementing the DVA's initiatives, emphasising the importance of realising value from those initiatives. Being dependent on support from cross-functional teams, which requires collaboration, the DVA must be given a full mandate enabling them to drive this, with the full support of the CEO and the ringleader.

Collaborate with key functions

Keeping relevant IT and business functions informed about the DVA's initiatives is crucial, including their role, timelines and resource requirements.

2. Contract: Securing commitment and alignment for success

Key stakeholders need to be engaged through formal contracts outlining their aligned deliverables. This ensures accountability for the success of initiatives driven by the DVA, who should also be contracted to deliver these successes, with clear value-measurement mechanisms.

The following concepts, managed by the DVA, will ensure alignment and robust contracting across the relevant stakeholders.

Demonstrate potential value

To emphasise the importance of the initiatives to stakeholders, showcase the potential value, referring to the content in Chapters Three and Four on value forecasting and the building of a solid ROI model. The 'Results' section in Chapter Four also covers an approach to 'PROVE' the value – generating the potential result of value extraction – to convince stakeholders that their focus on the relevant initiatives is warranted.

Confirm value attribution

Beyond forecasting, value must be attributed to each relevant function or stakeholder as part of the contracting process for value recognition. Again, Chapter Three offers guidance in this area.

Enforce accountability

Refine OKRs and revise KPIs to ensure clear accountability for value realisation. Every team, including data analytics, IT, relevant business functions and third-party suppliers, should be contracted to support the expected value realisation. The DVA is held accountable to ensure that value is realised.

Set objective: recognise value

To ensure that value is realised, the objective from the outset should be set to recognise value, which needs to be incorporated into the contracting. Refer to Chapter Three and the IFMAPI framework, and include the concepts for publishing value in the contracting. Focusing on value recognition as the objective helps to prioritise the activities required to ensure this transpires. The Data Income Statement is the value measurement mechanism.

3. Deliver: Manage alignment to assure value creation

The following actions, which need to be managed by the DVA to ensure that value is delivered, are crucial to managing the complexities of delivering cross-functional data analytics-led initiatives.

Engage with stakeholders

Understand stakeholders' needs, priorities and concerns and determine which stakeholders drive focus and priorities. Stay engaged throughout the delivery process to manage expectations and provide regular feedback. For more detail, refer to 'Demand management' within the SCRAPPAD framework in Chapter Six.

Manage the change

Establish a change management approach early and integrate it into regular stakeholder engagements.

Analyse broadly

Comprehensively assess current processes, role players, technology, OKRs and KPIs, data requirements; and capabilities across IT, data, and business; and anything else relevant to informing thorough planning.

Architect for value

Assemble a multidisciplinary team – including business stakeholders, enterprise architects, IT solution architects, data solution architects and business process architects – to design solutions that will deliver determinate (measurable) value. Instead of merely architecting a solution, the DVA needs to manage the architecture of value realisation, considering the interdependencies between various functions, systems and processes. The DVA's role is coordinating the experts, not designing the solution.

Factor in dependencies

Identify and communicate cross-functional dependencies in project plans. Ensure all functions understand their role and the cascading impact of delays on value recognition.

Implement in phases

Deliver value iteratively in phases to ensure stakeholder engagement. Break down any phase longer than three months into shorter, manageable segments, and ensure that value is delivered in short sprints.

Manage delivery tightly

To address slippage promptly, run a tight ship, maintaining strict oversight and enforcing an agreed escalation approach. Success in cross-functional data analytics-led initiatives requires world-class project management.

Evaluate, realign and reprioritise

After each phase, review successes, address weaknesses, and improve and adjust the plan according to changing priorities. Refer to the section 'Improve value' in Chapter Three, using the Data Income Statement as a transparency tool.

Essential experts for the DVA

The DVA will need support from various roles across the business. Key roles include:

- Demand managers

- Portfolio/programme managers

- Project managers

- Business process architects and improvement specialists

- Change management specialists

- Enterprise architects

- IT infrastructure and solution architects

- IT solution and integration developers

- Data architects and data solution architects

- Financial analysts/modellers

The DVA must collaborate closely with these functions to avoid duplication of effort. For instance, enterprise architecture can offer insights into people, processes and technology platforms, streamlining the DVA's analysis work. Support from senior stakeholders is essential to ensure timely access to required information.

This highlights the extensive influence required by the DVA and underscores the necessity for robust support and clear contracting to ensure successful delivery.

Do you need a data value assurance team?

A *data value assurance team* may have multiple DVAs and supporting roles. Consider your company's size and complexity. Large companies with many data analytics-led opportunities might need several DVAs working on different initiatives simultaneously, especially in complex environments. If your company's challenges are particularly complex, you may need multiple DVAs focusing on a particular initiative.

The DVA focuses on value enablement and acceleration, similar to how an enterprise architect orchestrates systems and processes. Some companies already have teams like a data value assurance team – we have seen them being called a *results delivery office* or similar.

The supporting roles for your data value assurance team should align with your company's culture, structure and operating model. If your company is service-orientated, the DVA can leverage existing experts such as project managers, programme managers and change managers from centralised functions.

While the DVA needs to collaborate closely with existing teams, avoid forming a team directly under them unless multiple DVAs report to the same function. Having direct reports could burden them with administrative tasks and people management responsibilities.

To bolster your DVA's capabilities, consider forming a dedicated team in finance or another relevant area. This could be a virtual, project-based or outsourced team, working closely with the DVA as their primary stakeholder.

The DVA orchestrates value across IT, operations, marketing, and finance functions. Creating dedicated teams reporting to them may inadvertently create silos, diluting their impact.

Given the specialised skills required, outsourcing your data value assurance team can ensure neutrality and force collaboration with existing functions without the team assuming delivery responsibilities. Outsourcing provides access to top skills and maintains independence. Resistance to external consultants may arise, but strong mandates, support and linked objectives can mitigate these challenges. Refer to the 'Support' and 'Contract' sections earlier in this chapter for guidance.

Specialist roles – like IT solutions architects and data solutions architects – should not report directly to the DVA, as they belong to specific functions.

A large data value assurance team will face road-blocks when collaborating with data, IT and business functions. They must resist the temptation to assume direct control over delivery and should remain an independent facilitation function to avoid becoming bogged down. Senior business leaders must support them by removing obstacles, using the Data Value Assurance framework.

Aligning on value: A unified directive

Successful implementation of the concepts in this chapter requires business leaders to adopt a mindset that differs from the traditional corporate approach. In many established companies, executives are accustomed to strictly adhering to their job descriptions and KPIs. Generating value through data analytics-led initiatives demands a mindset more like that often found in startups, where leaders embrace agility, innovation and a willingness to experiment. In these environments leadership teams work together closely to deliver cross-functional initiatives, being less concerned about their experience or specific roles and responsibilities. Generally speaking, in startups, the directive is clear: generate value, whatever it takes.

If your company struggles to generate value from data analytics, consider adopting a startup mentality for these initiatives. Encourage your teams to break down silos by prioritising the company's value creation above all else. In this way, you can move beyond the constraints of traditional metrics and embrace a culture where growth and value are paramount.

While adopting this mindset might feel like a significant shift, it is essential to remember that every step towards this new approach brings you closer to becoming a leader in data analytics-driven success. Your commitment to alignment and collaboration will set you apart.

Final thoughts: Aligning for value creation

On your data analytics journey, the real value lies in turning insights into actions that are embedded in business processes and applications, to drive measurable value. This chapter has emphasised the pivotal role of the DVA in bridging the disconnected worlds of data, IT and business to secure the type of alignment required to achieve success. This role is the conductor of the orchestra of your company's value-generating instruments, which are the various functions that must align towards embedding insights into business processes, creating a symphony of actions that drive measurable value across the company.

Revisiting the case study at the beginning of the chapter, on how misalignment destroyed value creation, having access to a DVA would have made all the difference:

- Given the proper mandate, a DVA would have had the support to align all the different functions and secure the necessary agreements to improve customer retention using the churn analytics model, leading to accountability.

- Regular and transparent communication up and down the data value chain of command would have enabled successful delivery, yielding massive value for the company.

- The roadblocks would have been addressed early in the process before incurring the eye-watering cost of building a fantastic data analytics solution that was never used.

With a DVA, you can experience the real benefits of your data analytics-led initiatives. As we have illustrated, having the right framework and support in place will mean the difference between success and costly failure. It is about more than just doing the work. It is about doing it the right way to drive measurable value.

As you move forward, challenge your company to adopt this structured approach. Embrace the complexity, align your teams, and ensure every effort is directed towards your overarching business goals. By embracing this approach, you are not just following a framework – you are positioning your company for a future where data analytics drives true value. This journey will not only lead to success in your current initiatives; it will also pave the way for continued growth and innovation. This will move you beyond the constraints faced by the 99%, setting you up to achieve successes equivalent to those of the one-percenters.

Key chapter takeaways

- Successful data analytics-led initiatives require more than just generating actionable insights. Insights must be embedded into business processes to drive decisions that create measurable value.

- The DVA is critical in bridging the gap between data, IT and business functions. The role ensures that data analytics-led initiatives align with and support business objectives to drive real value.

- Cross-functional collaboration is essential for the success of complex initiatives, and the DVA must facilitate this by aligning different priorities and ensuring all stakeholders work towards a common goal.

- The Data Value Assurance framework is a structured approach that helps achieve alignment, ensuring value is realised from data analytics-led initiatives. It focuses on support, contracting, and delivery.

- Positioning the DVA independently within the company, preferably reporting to a senior executive focusing on value creation, is crucial to avoid bias and internal politics.

- The importance of aligning the DVA's initiatives with the company's strategic objectives cannot be overstated; this alignment keeps the focus on driving value throughout the company.

- The role of the DVA must be distinct from that of a project manager or a CDAO. While project managers focus on delivery, the DVA's singular focus is on generating value, often requiring them to navigate corporate politics and influence decisions across multiple departments.

- Adopting a startup mentality, where the collective focus is on generating value rather than on rigid departmental KPIs, can significantly enhance the effectiveness of data analytics-led initiatives and the role of the DVA in ensuring their success.

A NOTE FOR DIVISIONAL AND SUBSIDIARY LEADERS

If you are operating in complex environments and relying on corporate functions or shared services, the role of a DVA is especially relevant. Implementing the concepts in this chapter will require overcoming specific challenges such as obtaining a corporate-level mandate for common objectives, aligning cross-functional teams within the constraints of corporate influence, and ensuring measurable impact despite limited autonomy. Tailoring these strategies to your division's context will be key to driving significant value and achieving success in your data analytics-led initiatives.

Conclusion

Congratulations on completing the first step in becoming a data-confident leader and establishing the RAPPID Value Cycle in your company. You have already accomplished something significant by engaging deeply with this material. Imagine how much more you can achieve as you implement these concepts and unleash your data-confidence.

Throughout this book, we have explored how data analytics can revolutionise your company. You now have the frameworks to identify opportunities to generate value through data analytics, deliver on those and sustain the value generated, breaking free from the shackles holding back the 99%. Your company can succeed where others are failing.

This is just the beginning. Your journey towards data-confidence is one of the most rewarding paths you can take. Every small step will build your confidence, capability and success. Use this conclusion to solidify the concepts we covered in the previous chapters and set an objective to continue learning. Remember, every expert was once a beginner. Your willingness to learn and grow will set you apart and lead your company to new heights. Engage with our community of data-confident leaders to stay at the forefront of value creation through data analytics.

The unique advantage for data-confident leaders

The gap between data value-savvy companies and those lagging will continue to grow. Some companies will keep succeeding. Others will keep struggling and, sadly, continue to be left behind. Companies that fail to adapt will struggle to compete, hampered by a deficit in data-confident leadership experience and knowledge.

Data-confident leaders who apply the RAPPID Value Cycle can help their companies close this gap. With your newfound knowledge and the frameworks provided in this book, your company is poised to lead. However, companies that ignore the importance of data analytics will face extreme hardships in the coming years.

As the digital economy evolves, the pressure on business leaders to be data value-savvy will increase. Data must be treated as the lifeblood of value in a modern company, as generating value through data analytics is fast becoming the norm.

Key insights to revisit and retain

To support your continuing journey as a data-confident leader, here is a reminder of the key themes we have uncovered:

- **Driving value.** Data-confident leaders are pivotal in driving value through analytics. They can either align with watchmaker data leaders to grow value; or challenge those spuddling data analytics leaders who execute initiatives like firing shotguns into the sky, hopeful that they will hit the occasional value target. This alignment bridges the gap between business, IT and data leaders, fostering collaboration and establishing a value cycle.

- **Balancing priorities.** The complexities of data analytics-driven value can be navigated by focusing on being value-driven rather than merely data-driven. Leaders must establish solid foundations and resist the urge to rush, balancing the need for strong foundations with quick value delivery. Data-confident leaders can move their company beyond the *We have always done it this way* mindset into a phase of dynamic growth.

- **Looking forward.** By focusing on value realisation, data-confident leaders can identify valuable opportunities for advanced technologies like AI to predict trends and tailor products to emerging customer needs, driving targeted marketing efforts and improving customer experience.

- **Providing guidance.** The data analytics journey contains a perilous trap. Companies that remain stuck in the transitional stage don't experience the returns they expect from their data analytics investments, and the value of the journey is questioned. Data-confident leaders can identify this trap and guide their companies to the strategic stage, where value is realised, curbing the loss of key talent and institutional knowledge.

- **Creating the DVA role.** The DVA is the secret weapon of data-confident leaders, ensuring value delivery by aligning cross-functional teams towards a common goal.

- **Establishing a culture of value.** A structured approach to recognising value and strategically investing in insights strengthens the vital partnership between the CDAO and CFO, establishing a data analytics value cycle that is central to business success. Data-confident leaders focus on nurturing the growth of their teams, fostering a culture where value creation is the primary driver behind data analytics-led initiatives. This focus allows them to accelerate solution delivery and sustain long-term value, even as they navigate the complexities of data platforms with robust cost-management strategies.

By guiding their teams in producing trustworthy insights backed by reliable data, data-confident leaders build the credibility needed to trust and act on analytics. The DVA plays a pivotal role in aligning cross-functional teams towards common goals and ensuring that every data analytics-led initiative contributes meaningfully to the company's objectives.

Our predictions: The impact of data-confident leaders

Business leaders will increasingly face pressure to advance data analytics-led initiatives, despite uncertainties. Data-confident leaders will play a pivotal role in eradicating wastage in this area. Here are our predictions for their impact:

1. The success of trillion-dollar companies leveraging data analytics will push business leaders to replicate similar strategies. Data-confident leaders can navigate these

complexities and drive success, even in rigid legacy environments.

2. Shareholders will keep pushing boards to invest in data analytics. Data-confident leaders know how to balance speed with building strong foundations. They can communicate this strategy to shareholders, guiding them to be driven by sustainable value creation instead of hype.

3. As we peak in the AI hype cycle, business leaders will feel pressure to adopt advanced technologies quickly. Data-confident leaders will identify value-driven use cases, proceed cautiously, and follow a phased approach to implementation, saving their companies millions in wasted, hype-driven technology investments.

4. Decision-makers' expertise in deriving value from data analytics and AI-led initiatives almost always needs to be improved. Data-confident leaders will guide investment committees towards measured, value-driven approaches, avoiding wasted investments and seizing the right opportunities for success.

5. The acceleration of technology adoption, driven by cloud-based solutions and their flexible billing models, will continue. As decision-making cycles shorten, data-confident leaders will rigorously scrutinise business cases, focusing

on value realisation and avoiding unnecessary investments.

Data-confident leaders are essential to navigating the challenges ahead. They know how to identify the right initiatives, what needs to be done to ensure that value is generated, and how to sustain that value by recognising and improving it. They avoid hype and distractions. Their sharp focus on value creation guides every decision.

Your next steps to data-confidence

Some elements may be challenging to digest, so here are important considerations to guide the development of your strategy:

- We recommend a second read to absorb the content in this book thoroughly. Additional resources to support you are available on our website (see **rappidvaluecycle.com**). Stay tenacious as you continue to engage with the material.

- Reflect on the *aha* moments and begin applying what you have learned. You might not feel fully ready, but remember, growth begins by putting these concepts into practice.

- Complete the Driving Results from Data Scorecard to assess your current capabilities. If you completed it before reading the book, you can compare your before and after results. You can receive a personalised report with scores in key areas which will help you identify areas for improvement. The scorecard takes just a few minutes. Access it here: **rappidvaluecycle.com/drivingresults**

Stay connected

As you continue your journey, remember that you are not alone. Many leaders like you have faced similar challenges and emerged stronger. You have a community, resources, and the inner resolve to succeed.

We welcome your feedback and engagement. Share your successes. We are here to provide support and advice to help you recover and learn from your failures. This journey requires continuous improvement to confidently generate value through data analytics.

Join our global community of data-confident leaders to connect with peers and find support. Join us at: **rappidvaluecycle.com/community**

Please share your experiences – positive or otherwise – by completing our survey at: **rappidvaluecycle.com/feedback**

Final thoughts: Driving value with data-confidence

What excites us most is the momentum data-confidence will build for your company. The decisions you make today will shape a brighter, more prosperous future. Keep pushing forward, and you will see your efforts yield incredible rewards. Do not settle for the status quo – there is immense value to be unlocked through establishing a data analytics value cycle. Challenge assumptions, strive for excellence, and seize the opportunities available in this age of data-confident leadership.

With leadership support, a focus on meaningful issues and a strong roadmap, your data-confidence can catalyse immense value. Who knows what impact your innovations might have on solving the world's biggest challenges?

We commend you for taking this leap towards data-confidence and accelerating value from data analytics for your company. This is no small feat – you are leading the charge into a future where data is your strongest ally in creating success. Thank you for joining us on this journey.

Yours data-confidently,

Karl Dinkelmann and Zjaén Coetzee

Notes

1 Wiktionary, https://en.wiktionary.org/wiki/spuddle, accessed 30 August 2024
2 Schulte, WR, et al., 'Predicts 2019: Data and Analytics Strategy' (Gartner, 26 November 2018), www.gartner.com/en/documents/3894082, accessed 30 August 2024
3 Ibid
    These appear to be the latest figures that formal studies produced. Until such time that valid use cases are established for emerging data technologies the value that can be expected will remain relatively low. Consider how, for example, concepts like Big Data that have taken a great deal of time to mature and yet still fail to deliver value in many instances.

4   Shewale, R, 'Big Data Statistics For 2024 (Growth, Market Size & More)' (DemandSage, 6 January 2024), www.demandsage.com/big-data-statistics, accessed 30 August 2024

5   'Why do 87% of data science projects never make it into production?' (VentureBeat, 19 July 2019), https://venturebeat.com/ai/why-do-87-of-data-science-projects-never-make-it-into-production, accessed 30 August 2024

6   Iyer, B and Davenport, TH, 'Reverse Engineering Google's Innovation Machine' (*Harvard Business Review*, April 2008), https://hbr.org/2008/04/reverse-engineering-googles-innovation-machine, accessed 30 August 2024

7   Lee Yohn, D, 'A Tale of Two Brands: Yahoo's Mistakes vs. Google's Mastery' (Knowledge at Warton, 23 February 2016), https://knowledge.wharton.upenn.edu/article/a-tale-of-two-brands-yahoos-mistakes-vs-googles-mastery, accessed 30 August 2024

8   Dillet, R, 'Verizon buys Yahoo for $4.83 billion' (*TechCrunch*, 25 July 2016), https://techcrunch.com/2016/07/25/verizon-buys-yahoo-for-4-83-billion, accessed 30 August 2024

9   CompaniesMarketCap (2024), https://companiesmarketcap.com/alphabet-google/marketcap, accessed 30 August 2024

10   'Google parent Alphabet reclaims spot in $2 trillion valuation club' (*Reuters*, 26 April 2024), www.reuters.com/technology/google-parent-

alphabet-reclaims-spot-2-trillion-valuation-
club-2024-04-26, accessed 13 September 2024

11 Hayes, A, 'Biggest Companies in the World by
Market Cap' (*Investopedia*, 22 January 2024),
www.investopedia.com/biggest-companies-in-
the-world-by-market-cap-5212784, accessed 30
August 2024

12 Böringer, J, et al., 'Insights to impact: Creating
and sustaining data-driven commercial growth'
(McKinsey & Company, 18 January 2022),
www.mckinsey.com/capabilities/growth-
marketing-and-sales/our-insights/insights-to-
impact-creating-and-sustaining-data-driven-
commercial-growth, accessed 30 August 2024

13 Wavestone, 'NewVantage Partners, A Wavestone
Company, Releases 2023 Data and Analytics
Leadership Executive Survey' (*PR Newswire*, 2
January 2023), www.prnewswire.com/news-
releases/newvantage-partners-a-wavestone-
company-releases-2023-data-and-analytics-
leadership-executive-survey-301711081.html,
accessed 30 August 2024

14 James, S and Duncan, AD, 'Over 100 Data and
Analytics Predictions Through 2028' (Gartner
Research, 2024), www.gartner.com/en/doc/
over-100-data-and-analytics-predictions-
through-2028, accessed 30 August 2024

15 LaRocco, LA, 'U.S. trade dominates Panama
Canal traffic. New restrictions due to "severe"
drought are threatening the future of the

shipping route' (CNBC, 25 June 2023), www.
cnbc.com/2023/06/24/us-trade-dominates-
panama-canal-traffic-a-drought-is-threatening-it.
html, accessed 30 August 2024

16 Hotz, RL, 'Mars Probe Lost Due to Simple Math
Error' (*Los Angeles Times*, 1 October 1999), www.
latimes.com/archives/la-xpm-1999-oct-01-mn-
17288-story.html, accessed 30 January 2025

17 Capoot, A and Blum, S, 'Google, Meta, Amazon
and other tech companies have laid off more
than 104,000 employees in the last year' (CNBC,
20 March 2023), www.cnbc.com/2023/01/18/
tech-layoffs-microsoft-amazon-meta-others-
have-cut-more-than-60000.html, accessed 15
September 2024

18 Shivangini, 'Tech Layoffs 2024: iPhone maker
Apple cuts jobs in digital services group'
(Mint, 28 August 2024), www.livemint.com/
companies/news/tech-layoffs-2024-iphone-
maker-apple-cuts-jobs-in-digital-services-
group-details-here-11724820182650.html,
accessed 30 August 2024

19 James, S and Duncan, AD, 'Over 100 Data and
Analytics Predictions Through 2028' (Gartner,
24 April 2023), www.gartner.com/en/doc/
over-100-data-and-analytics-predictions-
through-2028, accessed 30 August 2024

20 Karlson, P, 'Is The 60-Year-Old "People Process
Technology" Framework Still Useful?' (*Forbes*,

29 December 2022), www.forbes.com/councils/
forbestechcouncil/2022/12/29/is-the-60-year-
old-people-process-technology-framework-still-
useful, accessed 16 September 2024

21 'Conceptual Framework for Financial Reporting'
(IFRS, March 2018), www.ifrs.org/content/dam/
ifrs/publications/pdf-standards/english/2021/
issued/part-a/conceptual-framework-for-
financial-reporting.pdf, accessed 30 August 2024

22 'Conceptual framework' (Deloitte, 18 July
2016), www.iasplus.com/en/meeting-notes/
iasb/2016/july/conceptual-framework,
accessed 30 August 2024

23 'Steve Jobs: Great idea doesn't always translates
into great product' (Investors Archive, 11 May
2012), https://youtu.be/Qdplq4cj76I, accessed
30 August 2024

24 Deloitte Insights, The chief data officer in
government: A CDO Playbook 2023 (Deloitte,
2023), www2.deloitte.com/content/dam/
insights/articles/us176581_cgi_cdo-playbook/
DI_CDO-playbook-2023.pdf, accessed 30 August
2024

25 Stevens, F (director), *Beckham*, Netflix (2023),
www.netflix.com/gb/title/81223488, accessed
23 October 2024

26 Bersin, J, 'A New Talent Management Framework'
(Josh Bersin, 11 May 2010), https://joshbersin.
com/2010/05/a-new-talent-management-
framework, accessed 30 August 2024

27 Sabar, R, 'How Data Literate Is Your Company?'
    (*Harvard Business Review*, 27 August 2021),
    https://hbr.org/2021/08/how-data-literate-is-
    your-company, accessed 30 August 2024

28 Stevens, F (director), *Beckham*, Netflix (2023),
    www.netflix.com/gb/title/81223488, accessed
    23 October 2024

29 Richards, L, 'Counter-offer: a how to guide'
    (Intelligent People, 5 May 2022), www.
    intelligentpeople.co.uk/candidate-advice/
    counter-offer-guide, accessed 30 August 2024

30 Elberse, A, 'Ferguson's Formula' (*Harvard Business
    Review*, October 2013), https://hbr.org/2013/10/
    fergusons-formula, accessed 17 October 2024

31 Cameron, KS, and Quinn, RE, *Diagnosing and
    changing organizational culture: Based on competing
    values framework* (John Wiley & Sons, 2005)

32 Denison Consulting, 'Introduction to the
    Denison Model' (Denison Consulting, 7 August
    2019), https://denisonconsulting.com/wp-
    content/uploads/2019/08/introduction-to-the-
    denison-model.pdf, accessed 30 August 2024

33 Singanamalli, R, 'Understanding The Iceberg
    Model of Culture to Drive Organizational
    Success' (Empuls, 17 September 2024), https://
    blog.empuls.io/iceberg-model-of-culture,
    accessed 30 August 2024

34 McKinsey, 'Enduring Ideas: The 7-S Framework'
    (*McKinsey Quarterly*, 1 March 2008), www.
    mckinsey.com/capabilities/strategy-and-
    corporate-finance/our-insights/enduring-ideas-
    the-7-s-framework, accessed 30 August 2024

35 'Apple Revenue (Annual) Insights' (YCharts), https://ycharts.com/companies/AAPL/revenues_annual, accessed 15 October 2024

36 'Apple – 44 Year Stock Price History | AAPL' (Macrotrends), www.macrotrends.net/stocks/charts/AAPL/apple/stock-price-history, accessed 30 August 2024

37 Kahney, L, 'How Steve Jobs finally persuaded a 37-year-old Tim Cook to join a near-bankrupt Apple in 1998' (CNBC, 16 April 2019), www.cnbc.com/2019/04/16/how-steve-jobs-persuaded-tim-cook-to-join-a-near-bankrupt-apple-in-1998.html, accessed 30 August 2024

38 Isaacson, W, *Steve Jobs: A Biography* (Simon & Schuster, 24 October 2011)

39 'Apple Revenue (Annual) Insights' (YCharts), https://ycharts.com/companies/AAPL/revenues_annual, accessed 15 October 2024

40 'Apple Stock Price in 2012' (StatMuse), www.statmuse.com/money/ask/apple-stock-price-in-2012, accessed 15 October 2024

41 'REVEALED: The track changes aimed at improving overtaking at Abu Dhabi's Yas Marina Circuit' (Formula 1), www.formula1.com/en/latest/article/revealed-the-track-changes-aimed-at-improving-overtaking-at-abu-dhabis-yas.rejS8Xxbgoom5yPUInsek, accessed 15 October 2024

42 Joshi, A, 'Perfecting the 1:10:100 Rule in Data Quality' (*Medium*, 30 August 2021),

https://medium.com/grepsr-blog/perfecting-the-1-10-100-rule-in-data-quality-a1f31143f40b, accessed 30 August 2024

43 Simpson, R, 'Everyone has a plan 'till they get punched in the face' (Rowan Simpson, 2024), https://rowansimpson.com/quotes/punch, accessed 30 August 2024

44 White, SK, 'What is TOGAF? An enterprise architecture methodology for business' (CIO, 30 May 2022), www.cio.com/article/228328/what-is-togaf-an-enterprise-architecture-methodology-for-business.html, accessed 30 August 2024

45 Lee, Y, Madnick, S, Wang, R, Wang, F, Zhang, H, A Cubic Framework for the Chief Data Officer: Succeeding in a World of Big Data (Massachusetts Institute of Technology, March 2014), https://web.mit.edu/smadnick/www/wp/2014-01.pdf, accessed 17 October 2024

46 Tang, CS and Zimmerman, JD, 'Managing New Product Development and Supply Chain Risks: The Boeing 787 Case', *Supply Chain Forum – An International Journal*, 10/2 (2009), https://aquadoc.typepad.com/files/boeing-787-case.pdf, accessed 30 August 2024

47 Caldicott, SM, 'Why Ford's Alan Mulally Is An Innovation CEO For The Record Books' (*Forbes*, 25 June 2014), www.forbes.com/sites/sarahcaldicott/2014/06/25/why-fords-alan-mulally-is-an-innovation-ceo-for-the-record-books, accessed 30 August 2024

48 High, P, 'Zack Hicks Is Defining The Future Of Driving For Toyota' (*Forbes*, 18 March 2019), www.forbes.com/sites/peterhigh/2019/03/18/zack-hicks-is-defining-the-future-of-driving-for-toyota, accessed 30 August 2024

49 'Sam Allen' (Purdue University, 2024), https://business.purdue.edu/people/sam-allen.php, accessed 30 August 2024

50 Marr, B, 'The Amazing Ways John Deere Uses AI And Machine Vision To Help Feed 10 Billion People' (*Forbes*, 15 March 2019), www.forbes.com/sites/bernardmarr/2019/03/15/the-amazing-ways-john-deere-uses-ai-and-machine-vision-to-help-feed-10-billion-people, accessed 30 August 2024

Acknowledgements

We would be remiss in claiming that all of this is our own doing. Our supporters on this journey have played a crucial role in bringing this book to life – it is a combination of collective experience. Our teams of data professionals put in many years of hard work laying the foundational components of the methodology and frameworks presented in this book. We have forged our swords in the fires of the challenges faced by the many business leaders we have engaged with over the years. Our data analytics leadership network of mentors, friends, colleagues and clients have shared their incredible successes and challenging frustrations with us.

From Zjaén Coetzee

To all those who contributed to bringing this book to life, I extend my deepest gratitude. This project has been long overdue, and I am immensely grateful to my colleagues and counterparts with whom I have had the privilege of working over the years. Each of you has played a vital role in shaping the content of this book.

I owe special thanks to **Debbie Botha** for her insightful feedback and unwavering support. Debbie, as both a mentor and a catalyst for much of my success, you have continually pushed me to think differently and challenge the status quo. To my co-author and critique partner, **Karl Dinkelmann**, I am deeply thankful for your persistent encouragement to refine my writing and your relentless commitment to bringing this project to completion. Your dedication is inspirational, and you have had a profound impact on my personal and professional growth.

To my family and friends – particularly my wife, **Charmaine Coetzee** – thank you for your unwavering belief in me and for being my constant source of support throughout this journey. Your patience and understanding, especially in allowing me the time to focus on this work, have been invaluable.

Lastly, this book would not have been possible without the ongoing inspiration I draw from C-level executives, data leaders, and all those who are steadfast in their pursuit of leveraging data for good. Your relentless dedication to creating value and making a genuine impact has been a constant source of motivation for me.

From Karl Dinkelmann

Writing this book has been an incredible journey, and it wouldn't have been possible without the ceaseless encouragement, wisdom and contributions of many remarkable people.

I am deeply grateful to my co-author, **Zjaén Coetzee**. It has been a privilege to work alongside someone so knowledgeable and resolute. Your tenacity and determination were crucial in seeing this project through.

To our brilliant team of connected thinkers: thank you for years of collaboration, refining our approach, and bravely testing theories to uncover important insights. Your thinking has been integral to the frameworks documented in this book, and your ownership of your respective areas in Nexus Data allowed me the space to focus on writing.

Anwar Mirza, thank you for your unselfish investment of time and support from the early days of our company. Your encouragement to document our frameworks laid the foundation for this book.

To **Daniel Priestley** and the Dent Global team: your inspiration kept me going through the most challenging parts of this journey.

Zivan Trifunovic, thank you for bringing our frameworks to life with your diagrams.

To our beta readers: thank you for your detailed insights. Your pointing out critical gaps was incredibly helpful and deeply appreciated.

To my friend for life, **Phenyo Molefe**: thank you for always being there. Your support has been a pillar of strength.

To my parents: thank you. I come from 'good stock'. My father, **Richard Dinkelmann**, provided invaluable guidance and feedback, helping shape the book into its final form. I appreciate your close involvement in understanding the heartbeat of our business. I am grateful for your honesty and wisdom. To my mother, **Patty Dinkelmann**: thank you for your loving and encouraging words and detailed book edit.

Finally, to my wife, **Sheena Dinkelmann**: thank you for filling the big gap left by my focus on this project. While I receive recognition, you care for our home and three beautiful children, ensuring our lives continue with comfort. 'I love you' cannot fully express my appreciation for our twenty years together.

This book is a collective achievement, and I am deeply grateful to everyone who contributed to its creation. Thank you.

The Authors

Zjaén Coetzee

Zjaén is an award-winning data, digital and business executive with over fourteen years of experience in the telecommunications and technology sectors. He has led large teams of data experts on multi-million-dollar projects, consistently delivering outstanding results for South Africa's leading companies and government entities.

With Zjaén having been recognised as one of the Global Top 100 Innovators in Data & Analytics by Corinium Global Intelligence, and as one of the world's leading enterprise data leaders by *CDO Magazine*, his expertise is widely acknowledged. His achievements include the 2017 Standard Bank Rising Star Award for ICT.

Now a consultant, Zjaén helps senior business leaders maximise value from their data. His approach combines data strategy, management and governance with innovative digital disruption techniques. Zjaén holds a master's degree in computer science and a post-graduate degree in management in digital business.

Karl Dinkelmann and Zjaén Coetzee

Karl Dinkelmann

Karl is a seasoned data analytics expert and business strategist with nearly two decades of experience. As cofounder and CEO of Nexus Data, he leads a team of internationally renowned data experts, helping organisations unlock value from their data assets.

Karl's innovative approach has attracted global brands seeking to enhance their data analytics capabilities. His team's exceptional work has earned them a nomination for the Microsoft Data & Analytics Partner of the Year Award. With his expertise spanning mining, media, fleet management and financial services, Karl has a proven track record of generating substantial value through strategic data analytics-led initiatives.

A chartered accountant (SA) with degrees from the University of Pretoria and the University of South Africa, Karl is widely recognised as a thought leader in data analytics. By combining financial acumen with innovative data strategies, he helps businesses drive growth, improve efficiency, and achieve measurable outcomes. Karl's expertise and influence have earned him numerous accolades, including a nomination as a finalist in the Business Trailblazer category at the prestigious South African Institute of Chartered Accountants Chairman's Awards. His insights and practical approach make him a leading authority on leveraging data to transform business outcomes.